The Future of Human Rights

The Future of Human Rights

Alison Brysk

polity

First published in 2018 by Polity Press
Polity Press
65 Bridge Street
Cambridge CB2 1UR, UK

Polity Press
101 Station Landing
Suite 300
Medford, MA 02155, USA

ISBN-13: 978-1-5095-2057-2
ISBN-13: 978-1-5095-2058-9 (pb)

A catalogue record for this book is available from the British Library.

Library of Congress Cataloging-in-Publication Data

Names: Brysk, Alison, 1960- author.
Title: The future of human rights / Alison Brysk.
Description: Cambridge, UK ; Medford, MA, USA : Polity Press, [2018] | Includes bibliographical references and index.
Identifiers: LCCN 2017043970 (print) | LCCN 2017058092 (ebook) | ISBN 9781509520619 (Epub) | ISBN 9781509520572 | ISBN 9781509520589 (pb)
Subjects: LCSH: Human rights. | Human rights–International cooperation. | Human rights and globalization.
Classification: LCC JC571 (ebook) | LCC JC571 .B7558 2018 (print) | DDC 323–dc23
LC record available at https://lccn.loc.gov/2017043970

Typeset in 11 on 13 pt Sabon by Toppan Best-set Premedia Limited
Printed and bound in the United Kingdom by Clays Ltd, St Ives PLC

For further information on Polity, visit our website: politybooks.com

Contents

Acknowledgments

I am grateful for the opportunity offered by this series and my Polity editor, Louise Knight. I deeply appreciate the financial support since 2010 of my research at the University of California, Santa Barbara, by the Duncan and Suzanne Mellichamp Chair in Global Governance. UCSB doctoral candidates Natasha Bennett and Yunuen Gomez Ocampo provided skillful and timely research assistance. The thinking reflected in this book was shaped by dialogue with colleagues in a series of conferences and workshops: the North American Consultation on the United Nations Human Rights Treaty Body System, Columbia University, June 1–2, 2017; "Global Rights and Democracy," Liu Center, University of British Columbia, May 16, 2017; the 2017 Marsha Lilien Gladstein Visiting Professor of Human Rights, University of Connecticut, March 28, 2017; the University of Minnesota Law School – Human Rights Colloquium, March 3, 2017; the Roundtable on the Future of Human Rights, International Studies Association, Baltimore, February 22–4, 2017; the World Values Summit, Monterrey, Mexico, October 21, 2016; and the "Human Rights and State Sovereignty: Roundtable," American Political Science Association, September 4, 2016. Many thanks to the sponsors, organizers, and all of the participants in these conversations, too numerous to name but greatly appreciated. My contribution here has been especially influenced by constructive exchanges with Ruben Dominguez and the Mexican human rights community in Monterrey; David Forsythe, Daniel Whelan, Leslie Vinjamuri, and Michael Goodhart at the APSA and ISA roundtables; Christopher Roberts, Stephen Meili, and the scholars at the University of Minnesota Law School; the University of Connecticut Dream Team – Shareen Hertel, Richard Wilson, Zehra Arat, Kathryn Libal, Samuel Martinez, and Glenn Mitoma; at the University of British Columbia, Lisa Sundstrom, the Russia Justice Initiative, and Stephen Hopgood; and, at the School of International Public Affairs at Columbia, papers and discussion with Jack Snyder, Tonya Putnam, Beth Simmons, Ruti Teitel, Stephen Ratner, Felice Gaer, Yasmin Ergas, Sonia Cardenas, Anne-Marie Clark, the Center for Reproductive Rights, and Human Rights in China. The section on refugees in chapter 2 was published in a previous form as "Contracting the Refugee Regime," in Alison Brysk and Michael Stohl, eds., *Contracting Human Rights* (Edward Elgar, 2018).

1

Now More Than Ever

I can trace three generations of human rights in my own family. I am the daughter and granddaughter of refugees. I would not have been born had my father not escaped persecution in war-torn France and settled in the US – and his father had not first fled Poland after being beaten and jailed for labor organizing. I came of age in America with the rights revolution. One of my first memories is attending a civil rights march with my mother; during my studies I volunteered in a Vietnamese refugee camp in Hong Kong; and my first job was working in a women's clinic where we wore buttons reading: "Health care is a right, not a privilege." My formal study of human rights began with my PhD dissertation, when I traveled to Argentina to chart the fall of a dictatorship, the rise of transitional justice, and the emergence of a new kind of movement: Mothers of the Disappeared. After returning to the US as the Berlin Wall fell, I became a mother myself and began a quarter-century of human rights research that carried me from Quito to Delhi, from Johannesburg to The Hague. A generation later, my daughters have come of age riding the next wave of rights: one plots new paths for economic empowerment in Latin America, while her sister advocates for the LGBTQ community. What comes next? The fate of the next generation will depend on the future of all of the rights to protection, freedom, and dignity that have shaped my own life, and newer rights frameworks for my children and grandchildren – above all, environmental justice.

Human rights have fallen on hard times – yet they are needed now more than ever. Despite historic advances in human rights law and mobilization, unprecedented numbers suffer war crimes, forced displacement, ethnic persecution, gender violence, and backlash against rights defenders. These hard times in practice are matched by harsh criticism in theory. Nationalists and realists claim human rights are too much, development critics and legal skeptics say human rights are not enough, while post-modern, post-colonial, and critical-school feminists argue that rights are the wrong kind of politics for liberation. Human rights are poised on the knife's edge between hope and despair, beloved and beleaguered, inspiring and ignored.

But far from the "end times" of human rights declaimed by some (Hopgood 2013), it is time for a reboot that closes historic gaps and confronts emerging challenges. After several generations of measured success and unexpected shortfalls, the future of human rights lies in fostering the dynamic strength of human rights as political practice. People all over the world – from Amazonian villages to Iranian prisons – use human rights to gain recognition, campaign for justice, and save lives. With all of its limitations, human rights have proved a sustainable basis for solidarity in the face of violence and oppression. In this book, I will argue that the future of human rights must expand this practice to meet persisting threats to human dignity and craft new ways to speak rights to power. But, first, let us begin by setting the stage and defining the debate.

The Rise of Rights

What are rights? Human rights are a set of principles, values, and institutions seeking to assure the life, dignity, freedom, and equality of all people. Rights include both freedom from oppression and duties by authorities to provide and protect basic elements of survival, identity, and social life. They obligate governments but, when states cannot or will not protect their citizens, also other power-holders such as employers – and the international community at large.

These rights began as simple humanitarian perquisites often rooted in religious traditions, such as resistance to slavery, and developed further with the rise of citizenship and the ethos of the French Revolution as limitations on sovereign power: liberty, equality, and solidarity. Human rights gained additional scope and traction through Enlightenment-era social contract theorists of freedom and democracy, Marxian ideals of justice and solidarity, and Kantian notions of reciprocity and a cosmopolitan world order. The horrors of the twentieth century, peaking in the trauma of the European Holocaust, forged a new level of commitment to universalism and the "right to have rights" and generated the first intervention frame of genocide. While post-World War II decolonization and incorporation of the global South increased attention to the socioeconomic rights and self-determination principles planted in the Universal Declaration of Human Rights, they were then somewhat sidelined by Cold War US hegemony and political rights preoccupations. From that time on, successive waves of struggle against dictatorships, exclusions, and oppressions have produced a growing body of treaties and institutions to contest patterns of abuse – such as forced disappearance – and protect vulnerable populations such as indigenous peoples. By the 1990s, over two-thirds of the world's states affirmed at the Vienna Conference that, in principle, human rights are "universal, interdependent, and indivisible" (Lauren 2013; Jensen 2003; Iriye et al. 2012).

An international architecture for claiming rights developed in waves along with modern projects of global governance, from the Geneva Conventions to the international war crimes tribunals and associated International Criminal Court (ICC). The normative centerpiece of the Universal Declaration and the twin International Covenants on Civil and Political Rights and on Economic, Social and Cultural Rights are flanked by a post-war suite of phenomenon-based treaties, such as the Convention Against Torture, and population-protecting mechanisms, such as the Convention on the Elimination of All Forms of Discrimination Against Women. Parallel undertakings exist at the regional level, most strongly in Europe and the Americas. In some cases, regional norms exceed the global standard, notably in the inter-American treaties on gender violence, disability, and forced disappearance. An ensemble of United Nations monitoring mechanisms parallel the covenants in treaty committees – and UN processes go on to greater levels of reporting and potential responsibility via the Human Rights Council, the Universal Periodic Review, and Special Rapporteur visits. These standards gain traction through a combination of global legal institutions and jurisprudence, incorporation in national charters and legislation, diplomacy, sanctions, and aid policies. In tandem with these interstate channels, global civil society engages in standard-setting, advocacy, and sometimes implementation, especially for issues such as refugees.

Hard Times

Three generations past the birth of the international rights regime, freedom, equality, and aspirations for human dignity are vastly expanded yet deeply contested. Almost half of the world's countries are democracies, and up to two-thirds of the global population enjoys at least partial theoretical protection from arbitrary abuse of state power. The dismantling of legalized oppressions of colonialism, apartheid, caste, and gender inequity has liberated majorities on every continent. Intertwined with civic freedoms, recognition and respect for all forms of difference and dissidence – from sexual minorities to indigenous peoples – has greatly improved in many countries and is strongly supported by international norms and institutions. Global treaties, lawsuits, and campaigns on war crimes, contemporary slavery, health rights, and corporate responsibility have resulted in some consequential interventions – from limitations on land mines to access to essential medicines – that have saved or improved tens of millions of lives (Landman 2005). Moreover, despite cultural differences and political controversies, global public opinion is broadly supportive of the principles and proponents of human rights (Ron et al. 2015). Emerging research shows both that rights conditions are improving overall through cascades of rising standards and networked institutions and that some of the skepticism, ironically, results from rising expectations and improving measurement (Sikkink 2017).

And yet the glass is half empty. Sixty-five million people are forcibly displaced by civil wars and failing states – the highest level recorded in human history – and face a panoply of threats to survival, freedom, and physical integrity. Rising xenophobia has resulted in the illicit detention and deportation of migrants by democratic governments – and often hate crimes by their citizens – from Europe to Australia to America. War crimes in Syria have resulted in nearly half a million massacred, tens of thousands of political prisoners, cities of civilians systematically destroyed, genocidal attacks on minorities, and enslavement of women and girls – with no significant international response. One out of three women in the world has suffered gender-based violence, including femicide, battering, and sexual assault, at the hands of government agents such as police, criminals, along with private individuals such as traffickers – and, above all, their own families. Democracy has deteriorated significantly in many of the emerging Latin American, South Asian, and African nations where citizens had gained power from military or single-party rule in the past generation. Rising powers in Russia and China remain authoritarian, combining long-standing suppression of civil liberties with newer mechanisms of surveillance and repression that touch perhaps a quarter of the world's population – and even exporting these negative influences to trade partners and disputed zones. Developed liberal democracies that were rights promoters, however partial and inconsistent, have now abandoned all pretense of cosmopolitan concern – from Brexit to the populist nationalism of Donald Trump.

What are we to make of these contradictions? Are human rights exhausted – or resilient? Can better or different understandings of the rights regime point the way forward? And, most important, whether by rights or some other means, how can we – in the words of Martin Luther King Jr. – "bend the arc of history towards justice"?

Harsh Criticisms and Hopeful Responses

Critics of the shortfalls in rights trace their basis to inherent limitations in Enlightenment liberalism, state-centric enforcement, disregard of economic structures, alleged Western bias, and democratic deficit in international law (Baxi 2002; Douzinas 2000; Posner 2014; Goodale 2009; Gearty 2016). Thus, feminist, critical, post-colonial, and realist analysts each in different ways challenge the historical exclusions of human rights, human rights dependence on international law, the troubled relationship between rights promotion and humanitarian intervention, inappropriate cultural constructions and projections of rights norms, the bureaucratic politics and hierarchical status of human rights organizations, appropriations of human rights discourse by neo-liberal and security states to subvert empowerment, distortions of transitional justice for conflict resolution, and hard-wired political barriers to implementation (Charlesworth 2002; Barnett 2011; Goodale 2009; Stern and Straus 2014; Hopgood 2013; Tate 2007; Postero 2007; Meister 2012; Ignatieff 2011; Hafner-Burton 2013). One of the most grounded critiques relocates the rise of rights to the last gasp of Cold War liberalism, as it clashes with the contradictions of capitalism and US dominance – and, accordingly, dismisses human rights as "the Last Utopia" of bourgeois legal evasion of social justice (Moyn 2010).

One of the most senior scholars of human rights and world politics reviews and responds to this wave of critique with an affirmation of the progressive potential of rights despite limits. David Forsythe acknowledges the structural constraints of sovereignty, nationalism, social inequality, and double standards noted by Hopgood, Moyn, Posner, and Hafner-Burton but knowledgeably counters their distorted accounts of the history and politics of key human rights institutions – and their exclusion of transformative trends in the global South and grassroots campaigns. He concludes:

> the future of human rights is not assured but rather depends on human endeavor – agency as compared to structural determinism. ... There will always be political figures more interested in personal and national power than in the welfare of the many. There will always be powerful persons driven by the quest for great wealth and the status and luxury it brings. None of that is new. The basic question is whether the slow and complex building of countervailing ideas and institutions can restrain those perennial impulses. ... Those liberal ideas and institutions, which can operate to constrain the will-to-power of those who would repress, are not pre-ordained to succeed but must be reaffirmed and reinforced in each generation. (Forsythe 2017)

Moving beyond the crisis of post-war liberal institutions, this pragmatist response is grounded in a notion of rights as an evolving political construction – a contested basis for mobilization and empowerment with the capacity for counter-hegemony in a liberal world order (Beitz 2009; Hiskes 2015). In this progressive view, the legacy of human rights is to plant dynamic institutions and practices at the heart of global governance. The pragmatist Richard Rorty (1989) adopts a view of rights as a practice of "contingent solidarity." De Sousa Santos (2002) shows the value of human rights as a dialectic lingua franca across communities of values and identity that can come to play a transcendental role of an ecumenical global ethos. Goodhart (2009, 2016), in parallel with Zivi (2011), proposes rights as a toolbox of emancipatory claims and practices. Hoover (2016) grounds instrumental justifications of rights practice in a broader understanding of rights as a tool for the construction of legitimate authority and democratic political space.

In all of these ways, rights are an ongoing assertion of self-determination and solidarity in response to the requisites of power inherent in social organization, from the state to the family (Arendt 1958; Nussbaum 2000). This approach sees rights as sound in theory but skewed in practice and focuses on restructuring incentives and institutions to close the compliance gap and extend the reach of rights to the full range of violators (Risse et al. 2013). Scholars from this perspective recognize the changes and challenges for the historic rights regime in a multipolar world moving beyond legal strategies and grappling with new issues such as environmental change and information technology (Boyle 2012). Pushing past academic deconstructions of rights, they note that "human rights practitioners cannot afford to simply celebrate criticism and rejoice in uncertainty." Instead, constructive reformers advocate diversification of the rights repertoire towards a "human rights ecosystem" (Rodríguez-Garavito 2014). Summarizing a set of critiques that question the future of a liberal human rights project rooted in the middle class, a recent collection leaves room for hope when it suggests that, alongside the stark alternatives of business as usual and irrelevance (in their terms, "Staying the Course" or "Sideshow"), human rights may grow by embracing wider constituencies ("Pragmatic Partnership") and social justice claims ("Global Welfarism") (Hopgood et al. 2017).

A pragmatist, constructivist view of human rights *as political process* means that rights are not the answer – but human rights *are* the right question. Rights are the claim that we must ask of any social process or power relationship: Who counts as human? What is right? And who is responsible? (Brysk 2005). Rights are constructed through communicative action that includes treaties, laws, diplomacy, government programs, protest, information campaigns, representation and discourse – and the material resources they mobilize. Through persuasive pathways of empathy, reciprocity, and socialization, the practice of rights builds our identification across boundaries, our benefits and investment in cooperation, and our principles and expectations of justice and moral worth (Brysk 2013b).

"Universal, interdependent, and indivisible" rights are built through appeals to hearts and minds, roles and rules. Exclusions and dehumanization must be met with symbolic projection of voice and counter-cultures of solidarity (Brysk 2013b). Interdependence of rights and regimes must be rationalized and built, "making rights make sense" through rewarding roles in a liberal world order and linkages between democratic and global citizenship (Brysk 2009). The globalization of law, people, and information reveals and produces the connections between rights and builds an "indivisible" global community (Brysk 2001, 2013a).

Rights as Movement

The future of human rights is movement. Human rights is *movement*, not doctrine – a movement of mobilization, a movement of political process towards accountability and empowerment, and a movement towards norms of freedom, dignity, and equality. The future of human rights lies both in the fate of this process and in the ability of human rights institutions and campaigns to defend and expand rights claims in the face of evolving challenges.

There are three dimensions of human rights movement: closing the governance gap, expanding rights mobilization and mechanisms, and contesting rights resistance. The first challenge which rights aspirations confront is the long-standing governance gap between rights and enforcement. The contemporary world order is still based on sovereignty, and the international human rights regime is still anchored in interstate institutions. The rights regime was constructed to protect and empower, but protection has fallen under haphazard humanitarian initiatives, while the pursuit of national civil and political rights is assumed to bring physical security. This means that global governance for human rights faces a double-edged gap: between norms and compliance and between national citizenship and universal rights. Compliance has improved for core rights in globally embedded democracies when coupled with concerted civil society campaigns, but it falters in the absence of any of these conditions: domestic regime responsiveness, global leverage, and social mobilization. We will explore the security gap for human rights defenders in illiberal democracies that exemplifies these shortfalls.

At the same time, the state-based human rights regime still struggles with the "citizenship gap" (Brysk and Shafir 2004). As Arendt (1951) warned, those excluded from citizenship as refugees and stateless persons still lack traction to claim their universal rights. But, beyond these physically displaced persons, second-class citizens and those oppressed by authorities above and below the state become "people out of place" in the international human rights regime (Brysk and Shafir 2004). We can track these issues through the unresolved and growing plight of refugees as states increasingly evade or deflect their responsibilities. Moreover, second-class citizens left behind by wavering states and subject to powerful economic interests are also sidelined from access to international human rights.

The next task is to expand the range and reach of the rights system. This involves moving beyond the binaries of historic human rights, which aim in theory to make us "free *and* equal in rights *and* dignity," while in practice too often privileging the first-generation political freedoms of individuals. Recent waves of rights campaigns expand the universality and interdependence of rights by introducing new voices, delineating new rights, and mobilizing new access. The equity connection is enhanced by bridging claims such as rights-based development and environmental justice. The linkage between identity, dignity, and discrimination mobilizes marginalized groups such as indigenous peoples in transformative rights campaigns. Such movements also work to translate human rights as lingua franca into grounded vernacular and enhance the construction of global civil society (Brysk and Stohl 2017).

Human rights as toolbox must also move beyond the binaries of local and global, protection and empowerment, and insiders and outsiders with new modes and mechanisms of the regime. The human rights regime moves from legal accountability towards broader doctrines of responsibility via state due diligence, corporate social responsibility, and international community responsibility to protect. The expanding practice of mobilization has moved to new issues, new actors, and new functions. The international human rights regime has moved beyond law and top-down global institutions to multifaceted flows such as boycotts, rights-based public policy, and multiple layers of governance – such as regional institutions. We will review how mobilizations to combat violence against women show new pathways of political process and creative change in global governance.

Nevertheless, the expansion of human rights is a complex process that often encounters resistance and backlash – the movement may go backwards or sideways. The "spiral model" first outlined by Risse, Ropp, and Sikkink traces a dialectical movement of rights from invisibility to acknowledgment, from local suppression to multi-level pressure, and eventually from commitment to compliance. A decade after the wave of democratization, they find critical barriers in the diffusion of authority and the rise of counternorms and counter-promoters (Risse et al. 1999, 2013). The movement of human rights is now challenged by sovereignty exercised to securitize global flows and enforce social inequality, a growing gap between the demands of national and global citizenship, and illiberal hegemony (Brysk and Stohl 2018).

The future of human rights thus depends upon whether this decline of the liberal order and contradictions in its former champions can be reconstructed by emerging movements in a post-cosmopolitan world, which we will examine in the US. Even as the historic pathways of international institutions and cosmopolitan norms falter, citizen solidarity, resilient rule of law, and new venues of interdependence have the potential to counter contraction and foster the next cycle of expansion in a changing world. Here is where we stand: at the crossroads (see figure 1.1).

Human Rights as Political Program

The future of human rights depends on the construction of a political program to meet the evolving challenges of closing governance gaps, extending the reach of rights, and countering backlash. Human rights as a political program must aim to defend universality against dehumanization, interdependence against shifting costs and benefits of the rights regime, and indivisibility against shifts in the global order.

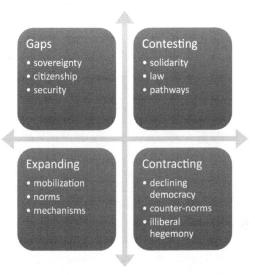

Figure 1.1 Crossroads of the international human rights regime

Here are some measures we can take to construct the future of human rights in a changing world, based on the analysis of this book:

- *Use your words*: The success of human rights appeals is highly conditioned by their ability to present resonant messages, articulated by charismatic or evocative speakers, framed by established rubrics of moral judgment, projected in accessible public or virtual space, and targeted to cognate audiences (Brysk 2013b). Information politics, framing, media, memes, and symbolism still matter – although their role and character has shifted. The classic use of personifying symbolism and bridging frames to overcome dehumanization continues, although shaming has deflated with the rise of alternative and counter-norms. Information politics has become more important to trace interdependence than simply to reveal hidden abuse. At the frontiers of speaking rights, we must craft new modes of appeal – from satire to patriotism – to confront the cognitive syndromes of rights resistance that have surfaced worldwide, marked by visceral anger, fear, and withdrawal.

Digital media and the networked public sphere facilitate the formation of movements and the viral spread of norms, revelations, and tactics alike, but they also bring new challenges. Online mobilization fosters "adhocracy" that makes movements nimble but often thin on tactical development and brittle in legitimacy. While censorship still plagues some struggles, in most cases access to media has become less salient than issues of verification, the use and abuse of information technology for monitoring, and potential negative dialectic as governments, corporations, hate groups, and trolls contest the public sphere (Tufekci 2017).

- *Follow the money*: In the past generation, rights practice has increasingly tracked the interdependence and indivisibility of social and economic rights, while also expanding mechanisms for market account-ability – such as boycotts and fair-trade campaigns. Moving beyond this, we need systematically to embrace the contradictions of capitalism and enhance the role of business as defenders of rights that create positive conditions for their activities. In general, bigotry is bad for business, globally integrated pro-duction depends on orderly and accessible migration, the information economy benefits from freedoms of expression, and many kinds of overseas investors have a long-run interest in stable and peaceful governance.
- *Use the right tool for the job*: With the expan-sion of actors, mechanisms, and modalities in the

human rights regime, human rights movements must be more strategic in matching problems to pathways for change. Even as global legal venues face new challenges, regional institutions are expanding jurisprudence, access, and coverage. Expanding campaigns for multi-causal issues such as violence against women suggest systematic assessment of the impact of public policy reform and value change alongside legal measures. Promotion of education or health rights may be interdependent with campaigns against discrimination. Increasingly, in illiberal democracies, we must think globally but act nationally to defend our beleaguered institutions as a prerequisite to promoting further global expansion.

- *Stick together*: The broadening of human rights claims and networks has been a key factor in recognizing indivisibility and deepening interdependence. Crosscutting constituencies for human rights are the best defense against backlash and resistance. The development of greater intersectional consciousness and practice in feminism at local and global levels is a good illustration of this kind of movement towards greater inclusion that also increases effectiveness, with linkages to poverty, security, public health, and intercultural dialogue.

- *Keep moving*: The history of human rights shows that struggles come in waves, backlash is inevitable, and forms of both repression and resistance evolve continually. Human rights as movement means that reflection, resource-gathering, and reform implementation are just as important as mobilization and advocacy – and that all of these facets are ongoing. Human rights are neither the end of history nor encased in the end times of the liberal cosmopolitan project. Proponents of human rights must engage in a dynamic political process to construct them.

This is not the end of the human rights journey; it is the beginning of a new stage, as we are bound together across stormy waters in a leaky, listing, but ultimately sound craft. This is no time to abandon ship – it is a time for "all hands on deck" to navigate the storm and plot a new course. The way forward is dialectical, dynamic, and strategic. The future of human rights is to construct a practice of global citizenship in a troubled world.

2
Unfinished Business: Mind the Gaps

In the spring of 2016, while teaching on an exchange in Vienna, I volunteered to help some refugee youth with their English through a local civic organization. These young men fleeing conflicts in Syria and Afghanistan had traveled overland to Turkish refugee camps, survived perilous sea journeys to Greece, and walked across Europe for weeks dodging authorities and harassment. Several had been students at the University of Aleppo and were similar in spirit to my students back in California – except that their homes had been reduced to rubble by a murderous dictatorship, with no response from the world or legal options for exit. I will never forget the lesson one Afghan boy taught me about the gaps that remain in the human rights regime as we practiced writing his application for asylum – which is increasingly denied to Afghans in the US, Australia, and even the EU. In the first draft he wrote, "I come to this country because there is a war in my country." As a teacher, I corrected the grammar, writing "I <u>came</u> to this country because there <u>was</u> a war in my country." But he returned the paper to me with the reminder "I <u>came</u> to this country because <u>there is still</u> a war in my country and I am not safe."

In a world still racked by struggles of sovereignty, conflict, and exploitation, the first task for the future of human rights is to deal with the unfinished business of the past. This chapter analyzes the inherent gaps that have become evident in the decades since the establishment of the international regime: the security gap, the citizenship gap, and the growing globalization gap. Even when the regime functions as envisaged for fundamental freedoms, it systematically fails to guarantee security, the rights of non-citizens, and protection from non-state abuse not governed by interstate mechanisms. In these cases, the right question to ask still concerns human rights, but we need much better answers. The gaps arise when, even though we have established "what is right," those rights do not fully determine "who is human" and "who is responsible."

The rights regime was constructed to protect and empower, but protection has fallen under haphazard humanitarian initiatives – while the pursuit of civil and political rights is assumed to bring physical security. The regime did not anticipate the decoupling of war crimes, democratization, fundamental freedoms, and physical integrity. Insecurity is characteristic of dictatorships, but it persists in post-conflict and democratic environments, undermining the exercise of hard-won freedoms. Stronger safeguards must be crafted, but state sovereignty, incapacity, and impunity combine to curtail the reach of rights. Similarly, the gap between rights and citizenship remains unresolved, since who has standing to access rights and the addresses of duty-bearers are still linked to citizenship. This gap has increasing consequences for "people out of place," whose universal rights are not reliably situated in state membership, and subjects of economic power with deflated citizenship, whose membership does not buy influence over the basic conditions of their lives. Thus, the lagging tasks are improving access to justice within states, fostering responsibility to protect across borders, and ensuring some form of leverage over private and corporate power.

While the security gap calls for more rights and the citizenship gap demands more justice, the governance gap of "private wrongs" requires more governance above and below the state. First, we will examine a leading case of democratic insecurity: the human rights crisis in Mexico. Then, through a brief focus on refugees, we will trace the challenges and potential responses to gaps in citizenship. Finally, in an era of persisting poverty and growing inequality, we will examine the globalization gap. In each case, we will briefly consider some current attempts to repair the gap, such as sanctions and transnational litigation. Later, in chapter 3, we will explore pioneering doctrines and practices of safeguards that offer the promise of more systemic improvement: protection for rights defenders, access to justice, responsibility to protect, and state "due diligence" for private wrongs.

Safety First: the Security Gap

The security gap is a combination of sovereign resistance, the lack of leverage over drivers of abuse, and a deflation of democratic accountability. Conditions of radical insecurity that contradict conventional wisdom are increasingly common. When states are recalcitrant, weak, or pseudo-democratic, the governance mechanisms of international human rights created to foster fundamental freedoms cannot deliver the basic security that was assumed automatically to accompany democracy, rule of law, and the presence of global institutions.

The first unresolved legacy that helps constitute the security gap is the persistence and changing nature of war crimes. War crimes are the foundation of the contemporary recognition of human rights, from the Geneva Conventions to the Nuremberg Trials, but they are considered under international humanitarian law separately from human rights, as a body of norms regulating organized violence by states against others that operates through international law, diplomacy, and reciprocity. In the twenty-first century, war crimes are ubiquitous despite declining levels of formal conflict. The nature and occurrence of abuses have diversified from battlefield abuses and treatment of POWs to more frequent situations of protracted occupation of civilian areas, the delegated detention of enemy forces and civilian suspects, the spreading use and targeting of a broader range of weapons, forced displacement, forced recruitment and the use of child soldiers – each associated with a broader potential spectrum of abuse. War crimes are interpenetrated with human rights abuse in ways not anticipated by the Geneva Conventions, as civilians are often assaulted, tortured, killed, and displaced simultaneously or serially by insurgents, their own governments, surrogates for both, and opportunistic criminal actors. War crimes are committed by a panoply of state, non-state, and para-state actors in ways that complicate sanctioning.

Beyond the gap of international humanitarian law for non-state combatants and state evasions of human rights through para-state actors, both systems lack leverage over abuses sponsored by outside states, fueled by resource flows, and enabled by the ungoverned transnational arms trade. Some of the mechanisms for regulating war crimes, such as peacekeeping, may themselves generate such human rights violations as sexual exploitation of civilian refugees. Many of these dynamics are visible in the Syrian conflict, with unaccountable terrorization of civilians by ISIS, the unsanctioned Syrian state sponsorship of paramilitaries and the use of chemical weapons, and forced displacement, torture, assassination, and denial of food and medical care by government, transnational, and insurgent forces alike, with almost no leverage over Russian and Gulf State sponsors.

The next facet of the security gap is sovereign resistance. Sovereign resistance to human rights accountability is routine for dictatorships whose power is based on suppression of their citizens. But, for these regimes, the movement of rights is ascribed to better implementation of the existing system of global conditionality, the promotion of democracy, and the last resort of humanitarian intervention. Human rights are stalled because protection is prolegomena to accountability and empowerment.

While such pariah totalitarian regimes still comprise a horrific threat to their citizens that merits much greater development of the regime change repertoire, the majority of the world's people now suffer insecurity and repression under more ambiguous authoritarian governments which usually possess some measure of electoral selection, legal institutions, and decentralization. Rights law and mobilization against dictatorships may lack traction, but power relations and potential leverage points are clear and mandate strengthening the resources and reach of the existing human rights system. Moreover, repression may actually be lower in some consolidated dictatorships where regime threats have been eliminated than in conflicted and unpredictable competitive authoritarian or semi-democratic environments where violence is a functional substitute for weak institutions. Conventional human rights monitoring, shaming, and sanctioning are much less effective in these conditions.

The conventional wisdom and democracy promotion regime of human rights breaks down when new or unconsolidated democracies continue to violate rights – or even take on new rights violations when conflict emerges or lingers. While, overall, democracies historically have better human rights records, there is now a significant cluster of electoral regimes with high levels of abuse. The deadly democracy syndrome that defies global rights governance and overwhelms fragile institutions includes high levels of international dependency, corruption, securitization, judicial incapacity, illicit financial flows, and failed sovereignty in rural areas, slums, and borderlands. Political elites systematically foster internecine conflict, persecute human rights defenders and, more broadly, civil society, distort media and information flows, and position themselves as regional powers or brokers of hegemonic interests to insulate themselves from global rights criticism. Elections become vehicles for populist dominance, clientelism, and deinstitutionalization, and citizenship is deflated and even denied.

Deadly democracies: the case of Mexico

Over the past decade, over 180,000 Mexicans have been violently killed – by a murky combination of state, parastate, and criminal perpetrators – and over 25,000 officially reported as "disappeared." An estimated 300,000 more have been forcibly displaced. Both the UN Special Rapporteur on Torture and Amnesty International conclude that torture in Mexico is "widespread" and "generalized." Mexico is one of the most dangerous countries in the world for journalists. Yet it is a signatory to every major human rights undertaking and an international human rights promoter. The country is also a democracy in the sense that it hosts regular free elections, although rule of law is systematically undermined by high levels of corruption and impunity. Indeed, less than 5 percent of these crimes are even fully investigated, and only 1 percent are brought to trial and legally sanctioned (Anaya and Frey forthcoming).

The citizenship gap is especially acute for "people out of place." Trafficking and femicide are rampant at the US–Mexico border. As the US pressed Mexico to outsource migration enforcement, by March 2016 Human Rights Watch had reported there were at least 35,000 asylum-seeking children detained in Mexico vulnerable to abuse (Human Rights Watch 2016). While a report by Amnesty International in 2010 had previously estimated that 60 percent of migrant women were raped by smugglers and officials en route to the US, a new journalistic investigation based on interviews with migrant shelters suggests that as many as 80 percent of women now suffer sexual assault in transit (Bonello and McIntyre 2014).

The pattern of perpetration and drivers combines repression of challenges to state policy with the state's pursuit of a "war on drugs," along with systematic criminal exploitation – and collusion. Using international comparisons, Mexico's military and police use unwarranted levels of deadly force and have been documented as assassinating civilians under the false pretext of criminal encounters, as well as handing detainees over to criminal gangs for exploitation and execution. At the same time, torture, murder, and sexual violence are increasingly connected to criminal syndicates' control of drug trafficking, commodification of people smuggling, and kidnapping for extortion of both Mexican and Central American migrants (Anaya and Frey forthcoming). Mexico exemplifies the patterns of "deadly democracies," as even the designated formula of global commitment, democratic institutions, and a robust civil society cannot constrain a militarized transnational conflict, zones of limited governance, and systematic distortion of the state.

Repairing the Security Gap?

Any kind of political change depends upon some combination of political will, incentives, state capacity, and accountability to both the global system and one's own citizens. While the international system has progressed greatly in the promotion of peace and transitional justice in the aftermath of war, the character of contemporary conflict often escapes state control or, conversely, fails to provide international mechanisms of influence over rogue states and their paramilitary delegates. The international rights regime assumes that capacity, will, and accountability all go along with democracy and global citizenship. From the guidelines laid out in the previous chapter, the most relevant principles would be "follow the money" and "use the right tool."

Sanctions have developed as the dominant form of international leverage over oppressive behavior by states over their own citizens. Economic sanctions may limit trade, military aid, economic cooperation, investment, finance, technology transfer, travel, or even cultural exchange with an abusive regime or entity. Sanctions may be levied by the US, the EU, or the United Nations, and in each case there are overlapping sanctions repertoires for human rights violations, terrorism, money laundering, nuclear proliferation, the illicit arms trade, human trafficking, and other violations of global norms. North Korea, Sudan, and the Democratic Republic of the Congo are leading examples among around a dozen states that are the subject of long-standing multi-purpose, multilateral sanctions for massive violations of human rights along with other threats to international order. Peacetime persecution of opponents by elected governments is sanctioned more narrowly by the US in Venezuela or the EU in Burma/Myanmar – coinciding with strategic interests (Masters 2017).

While comprehensive multilateral sanctions were credited with catalyzing regime change in apartheid South Africa, sanctions on Saddam Hussein's Iraq were criticized for their ineffectiveness and massive humanitarian spillover damage. Current analyses suggest that effective sanctions must target the material or reputational vulnerability of political elites who exercise control of the source of abuse, comprehensively include all major sources of regime support, interact with other forms of diplomacy or leverage, and contain graduated or calibrated programs for rewarding compliance or movement towards accountability.

Given this understanding, it is increasingly difficult to find "the right tool for the job" for the twenty-first-century security gap. Global governance such as sanctions is tailored for pariah states, governments may gain power through democratic elections without being broadly accountable, and middle powers such as Mexico, Turkey, and Russia are not materially vulnerable – especially if they control valuable natural resources or strategic territory. For the increasing number of formally democratic countries caught between "commitment and compliance," the efficacy of human rights goes beyond pressure from above and below; it depends on centralization of the abuse, as well as on international leverage through material and moral vulnerability (Risse et al. 2013).

The only scenario which yields political will to improve human security in a conflicted democracy is when two forms of incentives coincide: one of the drivers of abuse is limited sovereignty or internecine conflict marginal to state interests *and* the regime's specific basis of democratic legitimacy creates some level of moral vulnerability to domestic protest and international condemnation. In this scenario of genuine state will to suppress rogue perpetrators, international incentives can be created to build state capacity to control violence if political coalitions can be harnessed or created. The moral vulnerability linkage between legitimacy and rights may derive from a historic basis of state formation, national political culture, influential diaspora, or regional pressures that make some deadly democracies amenable to shaming.

For this reason, Mexico has been uniquely responsive to transnational pressure on a limited range of issues within the crisis, albeit sporadically and with modest results. The combination of extensive protest and Inter-American Court rulings on femicide has resulted in a series of policy measures, including investigations, the appointment of women's commissions, urban policy programs, and a landmark 2007 law on violence against women. Across a broader spectrum of abuse, Mexico has created a system of protection for threatened human rights defenders – which has been most frequently utilized, and only somewhat effective, for victims of local conflicts such as indigenous community disputes. The Mexican government has also attempted to provide some humanitarian relief and consular services to migrants, including facilitating interventions for migrant women suffering domestic violence. National protest and the Inter-American Commission on Human Rights have brought limited accountability for a few cases of egregious abuse by rogue officials, such as the disappearance of forty-three students in Ayotzinapa. However, access to justice for the countless victims of the drug war remains elusive – as the state simultaneously lacks traction over some abuses and is complicit in others.

Are these kinds of responses generalizable? There is some suggestion that post-conflict countries in which a new regime's legitimacy depends on international support and the rule of law may be amenable to an incremental expansion of human security, as may be beginning in Colombia. But the parameters of the security gap remain unyielding for most of the unforeseen deadly democracies, and human rights remain the first casualty of war in the twenty-first century.

The Citizenship Gap

Although the security gap is largely a question of responsibility, the citizenship gap founders first on the question of "who is human" – in the sense that full recognition still depends on membership in an institutional community, usually a state. The global order is marked by widening citizenship gaps in human rights coverage for "people out of place": whether physically displaced refugees, marginalized minorities and women, or bearers of deflated socioeconomic rights (first outlined in Brysk and Shafir 2004; see also Brysk and Stohl 2018). These are cases where the rights regime is incomplete or permits unsustainable exception, and current security and development crises are intensifying these contradictions. For refugees, an existing regime collapses on the requisites of citizenship, while, for other kinds of second-class citizens silenced by the interstate order, the gap is an absence of international norms to govern domestic inclusion.

Second-class citizens within borders may encompass women, the poor, indigenous peoples, and racial, ethnic, religious, and sexual minorities. In each case, systematic identity-based inequities in legal standing, political and social resources, and access to justice make members of the group vulnerable to abuse and impaired in seeking redress. In some cases, international standards transcend domestic marginalization – when they can be accessed. For example, indigenous peoples now have an internationally recognized right to prior informed consent for development projects that is sometimes honored by international rulings, multilateral programs and some socially responsible investors – affirmed in judgments of the Inter-American Court (*Saramaka People v. Suriname*) and the African Commission (*Endorois Welfare Council v. Kenya*), and in Peru's 2011 law on prior consultation for indigenous development domesticating the International Labour Organization standard (ILO 169), among others. But, in others, global norms are unavailable or irrelevant.

Parallel to the security gap in deadly democracies, the citizenship gap means that, even in democratic states that subscribe to human rights treaties, certain persons or conditions cannot regularly access protection, freedom, or empowerment. Women in many societies may be denied personal freedoms, property rights, access to education or employment, self-determination in marriage, and equal protection from domestic or sexual violence, both in law and in practice under discriminatory family codes, religious law, or sub-national pluralism (Hudson et al. 2011). The Rohingya Muslim minority in newly democratic Burma/ Myanmar has been subject to relentless persecution, assault, and displacement. Even in democratic European countries with multiple layers of commitment to global and European human rights standards, such as France, Roma migrants and citizens alike are systematically deprived of housing, social services, and due process. In China and India, internal migrant laborers are subject to discrimination, denial of social rights, and unequal protection from violence – in India, this is compounded by caste and religious discrimination. Indigenous peoples and poor rural communities throughout Asia and Latin America have been displaced by large dams and development projects undertaken without their consent and determined by international investors, even by elected governments. In all of these cases, democracy is not enough, and formal membership does not bring meaningful self-determination.

People out of place: the case of refugees

There are more refugees today than at any time in world history. An estimated 65 million people worldwide are forcibly displaced, the highest level ever recorded (UN News Centre 2016). Over 20 million are cross-border refugees, about 10 million are stateless, half are under eighteen years of age, and a significant proportion are women. More than half of refugees worldwide come from the three source states of Syria, Afghanistan, and Somalia. Around two-thirds of each of these major flows are hosted in neighboring, frontline countries such as Turkey, Jordan, Lebanon, Pakistan, and Ethiopia (UNHCR 2016). It is also important to recognize significant, long-standing, and abusive displacements in central and southern Africa following the wars in Congo, Sudan, and Rwanda.

Beyond official refugees, over half of forced migration occurs within national borders – and, as with official refugee flows, internal displacement is usually driven by war, dictatorship, ethnic persecution, and/or governance breakdown. The United Nations recognizes tens of millions of internally displaced persons (IDPs) who suffer similar vulnerabilities to cross-border refugees. Two-thirds of them are forcibly displaced within Syria, Iraq, Colombia, and Congo.

The Syrian war and the aftermath of neighboring conflicts in Iraq have played a leading role in the current crisis. There are at least 4 million Syrian refugees in the neighboring countries of Turkey, Jordan, Lebanon, and Iraq – over 2 million in Turkey alone. Around 6 million Syrians are internally displaced and face some of the same problems, with the additional burden that many lack access to international assistance. Around half a million Iraqis had sought refuge in Syria, so most in this group are now doubly displaced to surrounding states such as Lebanon. In a similar double burden, Syrian refugees layer on top of prior waves of refugees in several front-line countries. Jordan's long-standing population of Palestinian refugees now numbers around 2 million, and Lebanon hosts almost half a million Palestinians, putting additional pressures on humanitarian protection, labor markets, law enforcement, and community resettlement in those countries for the newly arriving Syrian refugees (Healy 2015).

According to EU and UNHCR figures, almost 1 million migrants arrived in Europe in 2015, about half fleeing the Syrian civil war via Turkey, with most arriving in Greece. That year the UN estimated that 40 percent were women and children, but by late 2015 the proportion of single women (including war widows), unaccompanied minors, and pregnant women seemed to be increasing. In the first two months of 2016, more than 130,000 individuals fleeing conflict in Syria, Afghanistan, Iraq, and other nations arrived in Europe – more than 55 percent of them women and children (UNHCR 2017).

People out of place suffer extraordinary levels of violation of almost all of their fundamental rights worldwide. Displaced persons experience assassination, torture, discrimination and ethnic persecution, both physical and sexual abuse by armed actors, state authorities, and smugglers, and lack of food, health care, housing, and education – and, of course, abuses and casualties of flight. At least 5,000 refugees died in transit to Europe crossing the Mediterranean in 2015, and almost an equal number are reported to have perished in 2016 (Townsend and McVeigh 2016). Police in transit countries of Hungary and Greece have assaulted and imprisoned refugees. A joint UN study documents gender-based violence for the Syrian refugees that includes wartime sexual violence in Syria; assaults, forced marriage, and trafficking in refugee camps in neighboring countries such as Turkey and Lebanon; exploitation by smugglers en route; and attacks on women in detention centers and open-air encampments in European host countries (UNHCR et al. 2016). Since 2001 in the Americas, as tens of thousands of Central Americans flee epidemic levels of gang violence and state terror and attempt to reach Mexico and the US, over 2,000 migrants have died in the deserts of the border areas (Smith-Spark 2014). Mexican police have also been linked to the assault and killing of hundreds of Central American migrants (Suárez et al. 2016).

The citizenship gap for people out of place is not due to lack of norms or governance institutions; in theory, there are plenty of standards for "what is right" as well as "who is responsible." Article 14(1) of the Universal Declaration of Human Rights, which lays the foundation for the global human rights regime, states that "Everyone has the right to seek and to enjoy in other countries asylum from persecution." The 1951 Refugee Convention is a binding document in international law, ratified by 147 countries, including almost all host nations. This treaty defines refugees' human rights, among them life, physical integrity, fundamental freedoms, the right to work, the right to freedom of movement, the right to housing, education, justice, and more. This standard was followed by an even more broadly subscribed but less binding 1967 UN General Assembly Declaration on Asylum and follow-up 1967 Protocol to the Refugee Convention and paralleled by 1954 and 1961 Conventions on Statelessness. States adhering to these treaties are obliged to cooperate with the UN High Commission on Refugees and to grant protection and status to refugees independent of their status in their home state. A 1969 Organization of African Unity (OAU) Convention further broadens the definition of a refugee from individual persecution to generalized insecurity due to war, civil conflict, or breakdown of public order – echoed for the Americas in the 1984 Cartagena Declaration (Jastram and Achiron 2001). The UN Guiding Principles on Internal Displacement and related regional standards in Africa and Latin America reiterate this set of protections for forcible migrants within their countries of origin, including the right to state protection from unnecessary or discriminatory displacement from armed conflict, disorder, natural disaster, and development projects alike. Internally displaced persons are explicitly shielded from detention camps, recruitment into armed forces, and forced resettlement, and they are entitled to humanitarian assistance, legal status, education, access to courts wherever they reside, and political participation.

One of the most important features of the Refugee Convention is the principle of non-refoulement – meaning no return to danger – given in Article 33(1), which states: "No Contracting State shall expel or return ('refouler') a refugee in any manner whatsoever to the frontiers of territories where his life or freedom would be threatened on account of his race, religion, nationality, membership of a particular social group or political opinion." The key right to protection against forcible return to danger is also guaranteed by the Convention against Torture and other Cruel, Inhuman or Degrading Treatment or Punishment (Article 3), the Fourth Geneva Convention of 1949 (Article 45, § 4), the International Covenant on Civil and Political Rights (Article 7), the Declaration on the Protection of All Persons from Enforced Disappearance (Article 8), the Principles on the Effective Prevention and Investigation of Extra-Legal, Arbitrary and Summary Executions (Principle 5), the European Convention for the Protection of Human Rights and Fundamental Freedoms (Article 3), the American Convention on Human Rights (Article 22), the OAU Refugee Convention (Article II), and the Cairo Declaration on the Protection of Refugees and Displaced Persons in the Arab World (Article 2). It is thus one of the best delineated norms in international human rights law. While the United Nations High Commission on Refugees (UNHCR) administers the Refugee Convention, the Principles on Internal Displacement are associated with a special UN Office for the Coordination of Humanitarian Affairs (OCHA). In addition, various refugee populations and situations are attended by UNRWA (the United Nations Relief Works Agency for Palestine Refugees in the Near East), the UN High Commission on Human Rights, the EU, the African Union, and the Organization of American States (OAS). Refugee camps, resettlement programs, and ungoverned areas are also managed by the International Organization for Migration, the International Committee of the Red Cross, the International Rescue Committee, Caritas, Oxfam, and a vast array of local NGOs (one report on internal displacement lists 500) (UNHCR and Global Protection Cluster Working Group 2010).

What, then, is the problem? Sovereignty is an important filter for refugee rights through states' power to grant asylum, but it is not the definitive barrier. The "UNHCR estimates that, over the past decade, 1.1 million refugees around the world [out of approximately 20 million recognized refugees] became citizens in their country of asylum." But, in addition, many states do offer various forms of "temporary" protected humanitarian status for victims of chronic conflicts and natural disasters rather than individual persecution, which are often multi-year and renewable (UNHCR n.d.). For example, the US currently hosts over 300,000 migrants from El Salvador, Honduras, and Haiti under temporary protected status.

The problem is not refugee rights in theory – it is host states' manipulation of who has standing to access those rights: "who is human" as a universal subject independent of citizenship. Within the sovereign right to determine asylum, even willing states use discriminatory and inconsistent standards. Currently, many European states grant nearly automatic status to fleeing Syrians and variable protection to equally conflict-affected Afghans. In 2016, the EU reached an agreement to return tens of thousands to Afghanistan even as it descended into chronic insecurity. Almost all developed countries grant fewer asylum petitions for individual dissidents from semi-democratic states than anyone fleeing pariah dictatorships, even when the asylum seekers fleeing deadly democracies document political imprisonment, torture, or ethnic persecution. As a journalist observing asylum hearings in Italy observed, "For the moment, a hierarchy of misery prevails: People fleeing well-defined conflicts, like the civil war in Syria, or oppressive states, like Eritrea, have a far higher chance of success, while the fate of many others can hinge on their individual stories" (Yardley 2016).

But there is a deepening and more disturbing governance gap emerging in the refugee system in the twenty-first century. Increasingly, at a time of maximum need, refugee-receiving nations evade their acknowledged obligation to offer asylum by undermining the international system. To fend off citizenship claims, host states resort to a combination of interdiction, deflection, outsourcing, offshoring, forced or induced repatriation, and deflation of access to asylum. Among long-standing and widespread filtering mechanisms are requiring visas from those who originate from the countries generating the most refugees, bilateral readmission treaties, "safe third country" policies, and the creation of artificial international zones, including borders and airports (Hathaway and Neve 1997). Each of these gaps has been expanded and extended over the past generation.

Interdiction involves physically intercepting migrants before they reach the border where they would retain the right to apply for asylum. This has been applied by the US to Haitians in the Caribbean, by Australia to North

Africans and South Asians off its coasts, by British naval forces in the Mediterranean off the coast of Libya, and by Spain to its enclaves in Morocco, among others. Upon apprehension, these migrants are either returned to their point of origin or detained – often in offshore facilities – and subsequently deported.

Deflection is centered on "safe third country" policies that limit or return asylum seekers to a previous point of arrival. EU member states have designated Eastern European states safe for migrants from the Middle East and other conflict zones, even when the states of first arrival do not offer asylum. The US and Canada have an official agreement that prevents an asylum applicant who landed in or was refused asylum in the US from seeking refuge in Canada, notably curtailing the claims of Central Americans fleeing conflict. Under the Dublin Regulation, EU member states can refuse or return asylum seekers to any non-conflict country deemed secure.

The latest case of deflection combined with outsourcing was a March 2016 accord between Turkey and the EU, negotiated by Germany, to redistribute asylum seekers. Turkey agreed to accept the return of asylum seekers from Greece in exchange for the EU processing Syrians directly from Turkey, along with billions of euros of aid and improved visas for Turks in the EU. This arrangement deflates refugee rights, since Turkey grants Syrians (like all non-Europeans) only temporary protection and not full-fledged asylum. Meanwhile, over 600 Greek arrivals have been forcibly returned to Turkey without an opportunity to request asylum. Moreover, the EU has lagged tremendously in accepting refugees that qualified in Turkey under this arrangement. In 2016, Europe accepted only about 3,500 – a fraction of the roughly 75,000 migrants stranded in Greece, not to mention over 2 million now in Turkey (Batha 2016; Gogou 2017).

The citizenship gap surfaces with brutal force in the Americas as well, where it is also met with outsourcing.

In July 2014, at the behest of the US, Mexico moved to secure its southern border to stem the flow of Central American migrants. Migrants from El Salvador, Honduras, and Guatemala are fleeing conditions of profound social disorder that have made El Salvador the murder capital of the world, and they often cite personal threats and abuses by corrupt officials, narco-traffickers, and paramilitary gangs. Between mid-2014 and July 2016, Mexico detained over 425,000 Central Americans. With inadequate opportunities to apply for asylum, and facing deportation pressures, less than 1 percent apply for asylum and fewer than a third of applicants receive it (Suárez et al. 2016). The US has pledged over $75 million to bolster migration enforcement in Mexico (Reuters 2015; Ribando Seelke and Finklea 2017).

A related strategy is offshoring: the creation of permanent zones of exception for the detention of asylum seekers that are not subject to national law and corresponding treaty obligations. The US has long processed Caribbean migrants offshore at Guantánamo (Rabinovitch 2014). France declares certain arrival areas exempt from its own laws, including some airports and port areas. Detainees in France and Belgium have complained to the European Court of Human Rights about prolonged irregular detention in exceptional transit zones with inadequate conditions, sometimes followed by illicit deportation of a migrant such as a minor seeking family reunification (European Court of Human Rights 2017).

Australia houses more than 2,000 asylum seekers in Manus and Nauru under horrendously inhumane conditions. In 2016 alone, an Iranian asylum seeker self-immolated, an Iranian Kurd was beaten to death by a local mob, and a young Iraqi man perished from a treatable infection when his evacuation to a mainland hospital was delayed for days. The accounts of Sudanese and Afghan migrants in these facilities clearly reflect flight from persecution and conflict that meet the international standards Australia has signed, but they are never assessed. Australia has given its former colony Papua New Guinea hundreds of millions of dollars in development projects but has housed hundreds of refugees in horrific conditions for over three years. In response to a Papua Supreme Court ruling ordering an end to the illegal detention, Australia refused to modify its lifetime ban on resettlement of Nauru detainees, instead concluding a one-time agreement with the US to resettle a handful of women, children, and injured refugees (Cohen 2016). Criticism by Australia's National Human Rights Commission helped modify the detention of juvenile asylum seekers in 2004 and, when policy regressed, brought renewed attention and some response from a 2014 report (Doherty 2015). After further court challenges, by 2017 Australia had agreed to monetary damages and to phasing out current offshore detention facilities – but not to accepting asylum seekers.

A final facet of the citizenship gap is forced or induced repatriation. State strategies to subvert their non-refoulement obligation may include collaborating with international agencies to declare a safe zone in a conflict country, negotiating unsustainable or abusive resettlement programs for a vulnerable population, or offering financial incentives and one-way transportation to return to an abusive or failing state. International declaration of safe zones for ethnic minorities during the Bosnian War of the 1990s and the Iraq War of the 2000s limited refugee flows but rendered targeted populations vulnerable to war crimes. Turkey was allowed to close its border to unwanted Iraqi Kurds because the UN coalition declared a safe zone that kept them in place. Recently, in similar fashion, Israel has induced the repatriation of a number of its estimated 50,000 African migrants who are fleeing humanitarian crises and failing states. Eritrean, Ethiopian, and Sudanese migrants seeking asylum have instead been shipped to Rwanda or Uganda, where they are often subject to human trafficking (Zonszein 2015; Harcombe 2016).

Rights Deflation and the Globalization Gap

While international rights standards grant ample attention to economic and social rights such as labor freedom and education, the impact of globalizing markets and rising inequality raise serious questions about whether human rights are compatible with twenty-first-century capitalist development. The accountability gap for private perpetrators of abuse is not new. In the era of colonialism, rubber barons in Peru's Putumayo and ivory traders in the Belgian Congo exploited, enslaved, tortured, and assassinated local workers. German firms were tried at Nuremberg for collaboration with Nazi programs of slave labor. During the Cold War period, corporate complicity with dictatorships was reprised by foreign firms targeting restive workers for repression or assassination in Africa and Latin America – from Coca-Cola in Guatemala to Shell in Nigeria. Such abuses were eventually restrained by the extension of state power to ungoverned areas, war crimes trials, and protest campaigns including boycotts, but new concerns surge with rising private power in the past generation of neo-liberal globalization.

The current globalization gap concerns a variety of ways in which increasingly powerful market flows and institutions may impact personal integrity, empowerment, and economic rights. Structural adjustment programs of international lending institutions may weaken state protection and social services for citizens' rights. Foreign investment may involve exploitative labor conditions, collaboration with repressive governments, or displacement. Globally advantaged investors and their elite partners may distort government accountability for citizens' social needs, political participation, and physical protection through corruption, manipulation of legal and electoral systems, and a "race to the bottom" to lower rights standards in order to receive critical economic support. In a related but distinct structural vein, critics debate the impact on rights of neo-liberal modes of development from market empowerment for some but precarious vulnerability, entrenched disadvantage, and competitive inequality for others.

Although all of these worrisome trends are related, it is helpful to sort them out for evaluation and strategies for amelioration. Overall, proponents of economic globalization show that foreign trade and investment may make development resources available to fulfill social rights, and the political stability and rule of law sought by modern multinationals tend to increase government protection of physical integrity (Howard-Hassmann 2010; Richards and Gelleny 2016). On the other hand, globalization is associated with a decline in social rights and an increase in inequality (Milner 2002; Apodaca 2018). Case studies of the political deflation of citizenship suggest that the risks and negative impacts for rights of globalization are seen mainly in labor conditions, supply chains, and forced displacement. Thus, it is governance of these problems that must be evaluated and reformed to improve the globalization gap.

The international rights regime has generated numerous mechanisms to address the globalization gap, including the UN Human Rights Council's *Guiding Principles on Business and Human Rights*, a UN Working Group on transnational corporations and human rights, and a Global Compact of voluntary standards subscribed to by over 3,000 business participants (Ruggie 2007; UNHCR 2011). Global financial institutions and some developed countries, including the US, condition finance or trade on business compliance with human rights standards on forced displacement for development, child labor, and the use of conflict minerals. The *Guiding Principles* have begun to filter into national practice through International Finance Corporation human rights provisos, OECD Multinational Standards that create national complaint mechanisms, and US sanctions on conflict minerals in the Dodd–Frank Wall Street Reform Act (Ruggie 2014). The flagship human rights organizations, Amnesty International and Human Rights Watch, have dedicated programs to monitor and campaign for corporate responsibility – including multinational abuses of labor and communities, information technology collusion with governments, discriminatory or coercive development projects and finance, and the pernicious impact of corruption on rights (Human Rights Watch n.d.). Savvy consumer-oriented businesses with image-conscious brands submit to monitoring of labor conditions and invest in corporate responsibility programs that sometimes substitute social services in weak states. Legal campaigns to enhance corporate accountability for human rights consequences of their operations have resulted in transnational civil and even criminal liability, from the chemical spill in Bhopal, India, to environmental health damage by Texaco in the Ecuador–Peruvian Amazon (Business and Human Rights Resource Centre n.d.).

But the governance gap consists in the voluntary and uneven nature of these measures, which is often outrun by changing market conditions and economic power relations – essentially unregulated. A promising arc of accountability through the US Alien Torts Act has recently been curtailed by limiting Supreme Court decisions, such as the Kiobel case.

One key issue is the increasing salience of illiberal investors heedless of even minimal and inconsistent labor and sourcing standards. China has undermined Western efforts to sanction Sudan for war crimes, contemporary slavery, and religious persecution, as well as violated labor and environmental standards throughout Africa and Latin America, while often outbidding more socially responsible competitors or local enterprises (Business and Human Rights Resource Centre 2015). Another challenge is the proliferation of outsourcing to diffuse supply chains that are difficult to monitor or leverage. Even within the widening web of accountability, structural features of political economy bedevil human rights efforts: extractive industries not subject to consumer scrutiny evade governance, resource-dependent states have distorted incentives to court international investors over their own citizens, and changing technology diminishes the bargaining power of workers. While standards and consciousness have improved, mechanisms have barely kept pace with shifting power relations – at present, the rights gap between individuals and global markets is even greater than that between states and citizens.

Repairing the Citizenship Gap?

Some aspects of the citizenship gap are more amenable to repair than the security gap, which rests largely in hard-wired characteristics of sovereignty. But, as we have seen with the case of refugees, lack of citizenship is still a hard filter for access to even the best-defined and subscribed universal rights. Clearly the human rights movement must triage transforming these costly systemic barriers, as well as bolstering related regimes for conflict resolution and democracy promotion. But it is unclear how further to construct accountability for people out of place beyond occasional situational progress in transitional justice or asylum cases.

Enhancing inclusion for second-class citizens is much more promising, albeit challenging. International initiatives such as improving children's right to a nationality and registration through UN campaigns addresses some sources of vulnerability, while transnational efforts to transform women's disparate legal status have made progress (and will be examined below). Above and below the state, emerging legal doctrines of "due diligence" articulating state responsibility for responding to private gender violence parallels transnational litigation for corporate social responsibility. In both of these cases, and in some successful protection of minorities, regional organizations and other meso-level institutions play an increasingly significant role that may shift the shape of the global human rights regime. This direction of movement does begin to close the gap of "who is human" and "who is responsible," using the relatively established platform of citizenship to define "what is right" – even as global norms and processes are increasingly contested. Expanding human rights ultimately requires empowering new actors, norms, and mechanisms. Expansion is a dialectical dynamic that usually results from a concerted campaign of human rights movements across multiple levels. We will examine precisely this process in the next chapter.

3
Expanding Rights: Bridges and Paths

That same spring, I renewed my hopes for the rise of rights through inspiring encounters with young activists from all corners of the world. After a workshop in Vienna on Gender Violence and Human Rights, a student from Mexico arranged a meeting to show me the anti-femicide protests sweeping her country in the "Primavera Violeta" march. In another café conversation, her classmate from Iran detailed legal campaigns expanding women's rights on the ground and web campaigns for personal freedoms gaining traction among Iran's youth. A few weeks later, a Human Rights Master's program in Bilbao drew students from a dozen countries – from Egypt to Nepal – each advancing struggles, from police accountability, to disability rights, to sexual orientation discrimination. While in Spain, I participated in another program whose very existence is a testament to recognition for indigenous peoples: a UN High Commission on Human Rights training institute for Latin American indigenous leaders, co-sponsored by the Basque regional government. While my indigenous students grappled with serious constraints at home, I witnessed their progress towards self-determination: building grassroots traditional authorities in Guatemala and Bolivia, defending territories in Panama and Colombia, expanding health and reproductive rights in Mexico, and reclaiming education in Chile. At the end of the summer, they would take their claims to the UN Indigenous Peoples' Permanent Forum in Geneva, a path-breaking global public space which I had attended in its founding years exactly a generation before – carrying a child who had recently graduated from college.

While the previous chapter showed the chokepoints that hold back the advance of rights, this chapter will explore some unexpected growth that points the way towards expanding both the concepts and practice of rights. While the citizenship gap centers around "who is human," new norms considered here expand the notion of "what is right." Meanwhile, there are contradictory movements on "who is responsible." The long-standing compliance gap chronicled in the last chapter and the conscious retreat from responsibilities outlined in the next chapter pull back, but, at the same time, expanding rights doctrines and mechanisms of accountability which we will trace here push forward.

Increasing understandings of the interdependence and indivisibility of rights reshape the institutional regime – and, if we are all connected, movement towards global governance may follow. Emerging claims for rights to health, water, and reproductive freedom bridge political and social rights, protection and fulfillment, North and South, and state and non-state sources. The political process of expanding mobilization triggers an expansion of the rights repertoire, standing beyond citizenship, and new mechanisms to deliver rights from global to local levels. This is the foundation of the "human rights ecosystem" recommended by Rodríguez-Garavito (2014).

Expanding rights means moving beyond the binaries of the core claims of the Universal Declaration: "free and equal," "rights and dignity" – as well as the poles of individual and collective. While both civil-political and socioeconomic rights have been recognized since the inception, rights campaigns have historically prioritized freedom over equality. Emerging movements such as the right to food and rights-based development can foster greater integration of equity in the rights agenda. Similarly, a broadened recognition of human dignity can enhance cross-cultural rights empowerment, expanding the repertoire of individual, adversarial legal claims to more inclusive forms of self-determination. This dynamic is evident in the instructive experience of the growth of indigenous peoples' rights.

The future of human rights also requires expanding our understanding of political process. Mobilization has moved to new issues, new actors, and new functions. Newly recognized constituencies such as migrant workers and sexual minorities enter the rights agenda and gain standing and access in institutions. The functions of human rights and solidarity movements extend from advocacy to monitoring and implementation – in some cases, even playing a role in governance. Women's movements run shelters, and rights monitors train militaries and corporations on the prevention of war crimes and labor abuse.

At the institutional level, rights are being constructed in new directions that complement the historic international regime. The international human rights regime has moved beyond law and top-down global institutions to multifaceted flows such as boycotts, rights-based public policy, and multiple layers of governance – from cities to regions. States are no longer just the target of rights movements – some states become promoters of global rights and role models for expanding the rights claims of their own citizens. We will specifically review how mobilizations to combat violence against women show new pathways of political process and the emerging role of Spain as a state rights promoter.

In some ways, this movement of expansion has the potential to close some of the historic gaps in rights – though in others it falls short. For the citizenship gap, expanding mechanisms for access to justice and broadening doctrines of state "due diligence" responsibility for private abuse could improve "who is responsible" for second-class citizens such as women and ethnic minorities. But the international system-level attempt to extend accountability for the physical integrity and basic needs of non-citizens in war and crisis ("responsibility to protect") has been less successful in bringing humanitarian intervention to people out of place. Similarly, the security gap – rooted in state sovereignty and consequent refusal to comply – is less amenable to redress. However, expansion of norms of "what is right" are beginning to address the security gap – at least in theory – by measures recognizing the universal "right to defend rights" and monitoring system for human rights defenders, including a UN Declaration and an OAS Special Rapporteur (UNHCR 1999, 2014). The globalization gap falls somewhere in between, with significant expansion of doctrines of responsibility but lagging development of effective mechanisms and leverage.

Expanding the Agenda: "Use Your Words"

At the level of norms and claims, the leading challenges to the exclusions and bias of human rights norms may actually become opportunities to expand the agenda to fulfill the original promise. The Universal Declaration of Human Rights states that we are "free *and* equal in rights *and* dignity," yet both pairs of concepts have become unbalanced in the generations that followed. The challenge that legal rights do not embrace socioeconomic and cultural inequity can be met by increasing the practice of interdependence appeals, coalitions of solidarity for issues such as labor rights and basic needs, and rights-based development.

The challenge of rights *and* dignity is the key to promoting human rights as a lingua franca in a multicultural world. We can transcend outmoded claims of cultural relativism through fostering the right to identity, the right to participate in culture – including cultural change – and a deeper reading of the struggle against discrimination as a right to the dignity of difference. We can model these modes of expansion through a short in-depth treatment of the experience of indigenous rights campaigns. A Latin American campaign summed up the agenda in their slogan "We are different – we are equal."

Another mode of expansion is to bridge claims for rights that cross categories and constituencies to expand "what is right." Campaigns for health rights, reproductive rights, the human right to water, and the right to environmental justice mobilize across intersectional lines of class, culture, political regime, and international institutions. They often result in crossover and spillover initiatives and frames. Some examples are the UNAIDS cluster of agencies that expand health rights and the emerging right to essential medicines crafted by the World Health Organization (WHO), Doctors Without Borders, grassroots campaigns of people living with HIV, and intellectual property jurisprudence at international and national levels. The human right to water is inherently both a development and a governance issue, with deep implications for health and gender discrimination – for example, when women are systematically attacked because of inadequate access to sanitation. Campaigns against human trafficking combine issues of freedom, migration, labor rights, gender, children's rights – and often other forms of discrimination, as victims of trafficking are often from marginalized ethnic or caste groups.

Expanding interdependence: rights-based development

The emergence of rights-based development illustrates the transformative power of expanding rights for interdependence and empowerment. Leading NGOs such as Oxfam adopted the rubric of rights-based development to deepen local ownership and promote participatory, sustainable development models. At the same time, by the 1990s traditional human rights advocates, from a landmark campaign by Human Rights Watch for indigenous land rights to Amnesty International coalitions to combat persecution of environmental defenders, embraced an analysis of development conflict as a root cause and interdependent driver of abuse (Nelson and Dorsey 2008). The 2000 Human Development Report published by the UN Development Programme, entitled *Human Rights and Human Development*, also heralded this shift, with concurrent development of human security indicators and responsibilities.

As a consequence, doctrines and assessments of rights-based development generate a deeper level of critique for the impact of international development funders and institutions such as the World Bank and foreign aid agencies. At the same time, rights expand and gain traction as the collective human right to development – previously declared as a UN standard and invoked mainly by postcolonial states as a principle of the world economic order – becomes a concrete claim of rights by specific communities affected by transnational, national, and local actors alike. Development becomes redefined by rights mobilization from the generation of capital and resources to a human-centered promotion of capabilities and access to such essential needs as water, health, and education. This movement of rights bridges economic and social rights with political empowerment and discrimination and, at the same time, transcends the false distinction between negative/non-interference and positive/provision rights, holding the state to a higher standard of fulfillment than mere compliance. Furthermore, these crossover rights implicate transparency and corruption as human rights violations. By the first decade of the twenty-first century, around 10 percent of OECD foreign aid budgets had moved to civil and political rights projects – fostering development by funding rights (Kindornay et al. 2012).

Development rights move from treaty compliance, to provision of development programming, to mobilization of affected constituencies around new frames, to a basis for local litigation. Aid providers such as the UK Department for International Development and even the US CARE have been influenced by rights-based development to focus to a greater extent on inclusion, a more holistic assessment of the impact of development, and social analysis of power relations; CARE refers to "Rights, Roots, and Responsibilities." Development actors such as Oxfam now explicitly promote advocacy and empowerment in partner communities as a development rights outcome – and even sponsor local grassroots mobilization (Cornwall and Nyamu-Mesembi 2004). Movements and litigation for the right to food in India, housing in South Africa, or AIDS drugs in Brazil illustrate some of the potential opened by this new thinking (Gauri and Gloppen 2012). Transnational litigation against oil and mining companies in Nigeria, Papua New Guinea, and Ecuador advances crosscutting claims to local consultation, labor rights, and environmental justice. Crosscutting campaigns on issues such as conflict minerals and child soldiers combine the mobilization and framing power of human rights, development, and conflict resolution NGOs, grassroots movements, and foreign policy actors.

Expanding voice: the case of indigenous peoples

In the past generation, indigenous people – the original inhabitants of the citizenship gap – have expanded voices and spaces for rights claims significantly. Although their claims have not always availed, their presence has transformed the character of the international system and the repertoire of rights. The emergence of worldwide indigenous movements, with special strength in Latin America, has resulted in new international norms, constitutional and legal rights in dozens of states, land grants and autonomous zones, standing in development and environmental governance, recognition of customary law and alternative justice systems in some countries, and numerous programs for development, conservation, and cultural preservation in indigenous communities. These measures have been tremendously uneven in adoption and impact, hotly contested, and sometimes overshadowed by new threats to the survival of indigenous communities – but they have protected lives, shifted power relations, and empowered previously marginalized citizens. From autonomous areas in Mexico to protected territories in Brazil, from indigenous political parties in Ecuador to tribal development schemes in India, from World Bank standards on forced displacement to self-government in Canada, indigenous rights make a difference in the fate of millions (Brysk 2000; Inguanzo and Wright 2016).

The centerpiece of the new international indigenous rights norms is the 2007 United Nations Declaration on the Rights of Indigenous Peoples (UNDRIP), which transcends the earlier assimilationist and protective International Labor Organization Convention 107. The UNDRIP, endorsed by 144 states, is considered a step towards the decolonization of law and the movement of indigenous peoples to subjects (Meijknecht 2001; Sambo Dorough 2009: 265). The new norm is notable for expanding recognition of collective and cultural rights, the right to development, a broadened notion of land and resource rights to ancestral "territory," and a drafting process that included over a decade of annual meetings in a Working Group (later Permanent Forum) on Indigenous Peoples accessible to hundreds of non-governmental representatives of indigenous peoples alongside state parties and experts. An additional rights innovation is the recognition of the need for free, prior, and informed consent of indigenous peoples when states take legislative or administrative measures that may affect them (see Rombouts 2014; Article 19 of the UNDRIP). The Indigenous Rights Declaration also builds the rights repertoire for recognition of historical injustices as an impediment to the enjoyment of human rights and contains a number of provisions on the right of redress for indigenous peoples (Gómez Isa 2017). The broader context of international and national recognition of indigenous rights also incorporates expansions of the notion of environmental rights, multicultural citizenship, and the abuse frame of "ethnocide" – the systematic cultural destruction of a community that may or may not include physical genocide.

The indigenous rights regime is implemented by a variety of mechanisms. At the UN level, the Permanent Forum on Indigenous Issues uses the UNDRIP as its legal framework, while various UN bodies such as the High Commission on Human Rights and UNICEF are increasingly using it as a parameter of reference when interpreting international legal standards and their mandates. There is an investigatory Special Rapporteur on human rights of indigenous peoples at both the UN and the OAS, an Expert Mechanism on the Rights of Indigenous Peoples (EMRIP), and a number of landmark rulings of the Inter-American Court of Human Rights for indigenous peoples' land rights, autonomy, and reparations for political violence. At the national level, the Colombian Constitutional Court, the Constitutional Court of Peru, and the Supreme Court of Belize have used the UNDRIP in some of their decisions. In Bolivia, a law was adopted explicitly to incorporate the declaration in its domestic legal system (Gómez Isa 2017).

Expanding claims: environmental justice

Expanding claims for environmental justice are a powerful response to the challenges of the current generation of human rights that will shape the future. While the late twentieth-century norms included a generalized "right to a safe environment" with limited obligations by states, twenty-first-century crisis has stimulated clarification and recognition of global environmental rights as a form of intergenerational justice (Nickel 1993; Hiskes 2015).

Pollution, depletion of essential resources such as water, climate change, and loss of biodiversity threaten humans' rights to life, health, housing, livelihood, and, in some cases, cultural identity (for indigenous peoples, among others). Threats to a safe environment often intersect with other forms of social disadvantage or discrimination, as when pollution is dumped in poor communities or when development patterns that privilege elite countries and sectors generate climate change that displaces the most vulnerable from marginal areas for habitation and agriculture. But even beyond this, the globalization of environmental justice claims by indigenous advocates has enlarged the frame from equity to a broader notion of the right to environmental conditions that support their rights to recognition, collective cultural reproduction, and the development of capabilities (Schlosberg and Carruthers 2010).

Among dimensions of environmental rights that expand the agenda and mobilize campaigns are environmental racism/discrimination, the forced displacement of climate refugees, and the protection of environmental defenders. Environmental racism includes domestic patterns within developed countries such as water contamination in Flint, Michigan, as well as global inequities such as the export of toxic waste from the EU to Nigeria. Climate refugees are residents fleeing low-lying flood-prone, desertified, or disaster-affected areas rendered uninhabitable by development, consumption, and policy patterns beyond their control. Entire Pacific islands with insufficient global bargaining power to constrain global consumption fostering rises in sea levels are forced to evacuate to Australia, while New Orleans residents driven out by Hurricane Katrina were thrice victimized by their government, in discriminatory infrastructure development, negation of climate change recognition and cooperation, and disparate disaster response to communities of color. It is estimated that up to 2 billion people could be displaced by climate change by 2100 (Scotti 2017) – with tremendous implications for social conflict, poverty, and citizenship. All of these issues politicize the distribution of the costs and benefits of development, demand greater citizen control of critical life conditions, and try to extend "who is responsible."

The protection of environmental defenders brings together fundamental freedoms to claim and mobilize for rights with the extension of rights claims to development processes and public policies at the national and global scale. Every year in this generation, hundreds of advocates for environmental justice have paid with their lives, from park rangers in protected areas such as the DRC's Virunga to whistleblowers on illicit Amazon mining, with scores targeted in Brazil, Colombia, and the Philippines (The Guardian 2017). Global Witness, Human Rights Watch, and the Sierra Club have programs to monitor and mobilize for the protection of environmental rights defenders. The assassination and harassment of environmental defenders highlight the security side of environmental justice, which depends on state protection and accountability – as with other aspects of contested development, often confounded by corruption and complicity with private perpetrators.

International initiatives that seek to fulfill environmental justice claims include a United Nations Special Rapporteur, the incorporation of environmental damages in many of the indigenous rights and corporate responsibility litigations cited above, and joint campaigns by rights and environmental organizations. In 2011 the UN Human Rights Council designated a Special Rapporteur on the Rights to a Safe Environment who traces the human rights implications of biodiversity and ecosystem vulnerability. He has begun regional workshops for rights-based environmental legal accountability and established a web portal with resources for environmental defenders (Human Rights Council 2017). But norms have expanded more than tools, as environmental justice falls in the globalization gap.

Expanding the Reach of Rights: "Use the Right Tool for the Job"

Once the agenda has been extended to new actors and claims, we turn to expanding processes and institutions to enhance the reach of rights. Human rights have progressed from being a legal doctrine to become a worldwide movement that embraces widening issues and constituencies and now plays multiple roles, from monitoring, to advocacy, to social transformation, to implementation. This involves a combination of building the toolbox and expanding "who is responsible." This chapter will chart these developments through the expansion of global governance to combat violence against women.

Movements to expand the reach of rights for new problems and populations propose new responsibilities for their fulfillment. Violence against women demands due diligence accountability for non-state perpetrators, while transnational labor rights violations catalyze doctrines of corporate social responsibility. The due diligence doctrine has reshaped jurisprudence in Europe and Latin America and has helped to support claims of gender-based asylum worldwide. Corporate social responsibility has produced monitoring regimes, the UN Global Compact, and transnational litigation against corporations for violations of labor rights and complicity in state coercion. Between states, and when governance collapses as a result of war, natural disasters, or health emergency, there is a globally recognized "responsibility to protect" – a humanitarian safety net. Despite extensive elaboration in UN resolutions and orientation of fulfillment through OCHA and the Human Security Network of over a dozen states, the latter doctrine has unfortunately been more important as a conceptual horizon than practice.

The repertoire available to meet those expanded responsibilities has also grown. The human rights regime itself has expanded from top-down global organizations to horizontal, regional, and transnational institutions, and human rights have been incorporated across other global governance structures, from the World Bank to global health forums. Trickling down, rights extend to independent national entities such as ombudsman offices and National Human Rights Institutions (Cardenas 2014), as well as purposive intergovernmental promoters such as the Organization for Security and Co-operation in Europe (OSCE). Meso-level regional organizations, human rights commissions, and courts forge ahead, especially in the Americas and Europe, with norms that often exceed the global benchmark on forced disappearance, violence against women, and indigenous rights, among others. Some states even take on roles as human rights promoters, whether as system-wide "global good Samaritans" or as issue leaders, as with Sweden's feminist foreign policy. Rights are translated at the subnational region level in major developing countries such as Mexico, India, and Nigeria, while worldwide rights are localized by hundreds of human rights cities. Circling back to the international level, all of these movements result in more treaty bodies, Special Rapporteurs, thematic conferences and programs, and the peer-level Universal Periodic Review of state practices by the UN Human Rights Commission. From the recent Convention on the Rights of Domestic Workers to the UN Special Rapporteur on the Right to Food, from landmark conferences on femicide to the International Criminal Court Trust Fund for Victims, the rights regime expands institutional responses to ever-widening circles of the human condition and power relations.

To meet the range of expanded responsibilities with the new toolbox, human rights broadens the political process. First, from its roots in law, human rights grow to a dialectical mobilization of transnational networks and grassroots groups – from above and below. Mobilization moves from monitoring, to advocacy, to fulfillment, as human rights organizations rescue refugees or process asylum cases. Options to "follow the money" proliferate from state-based international sanctions to boycott campaigns, fair-trade initiatives, socially responsible investment filters and firms, corporate social responsibility practices, and the establishment of "social enterprise" to fulfill economic and social rights (ECSR). Information politics develops from "naming and shaming" to a widely disseminated global flow of grassroots monitoring, information campaigns, shadow reports to international bodies, and a new wave of human rights organizations and practices dedicated to informational empowerment (such as media training by Global Witness).

Expanding options: the case of violence against women

Violence against women is arguably the world's largest human rights problem, estimated to affect one out of three women worldwide – around a billion people. While gender violence remains a complex, deeply rooted, and pervasive problem, human rights frames and mobilizations for a social problem that was formerly naturalized as personal and cultural have produced a dramatic increase in policies and resources at the global, regional, and national levels. The following is based on an extended study of global responses (Brysk, forthcoming).

After decades of growing awareness and transnational women's movement mobilization, the 1993 Vienna World Conference on Human Rights declared that "women's rights are human rights" and discussed gender violence as a global problem. The following year in Beijing, the Fourth World Conference on Women also made violence against women a central issue. Accordingly, in 1993, the UN issued a Declaration on the Elimination of Violence Against Women that was adopted by consensus. Article 2 of the declaration provides a comprehensive global standard defining both public and private forms of violence: physical and sexual violence in the family, community, and state, including battering, rape, harmful traditional practices, exploitation, harassment, and trafficking. In 2000, the landmark UN Security Council Resolution 1325 on Women, Peace and Security acknowledged the gendered impact of war on women, urged special measures to protect them – especially from sexual violence – and mandated increased participation by women in all global institutions and conflict resolution processes.

Expanding human rights to confront gender violence, activists and international law initially extended the discrimination standards of the Convention on the Elimination of All Forms of Discrimination Against Women (CEDAW) and framed violence – especially traditional practices such as FGM/C – as a barrier to the exercise of established civil and political rights and freedoms. During the 1990s, understandings of women's right to security expanded further, as patterns of wartime rape and fatal domestic violence were taken up by mainstream human rights organizations such as Human Rights Watch and regional institutions such as the Inter-American Human Rights Convention. As a result, "what is right" is applied to both private and public gender violence. Sexual assault by state actors is bridged to the established human rights norms of physical integrity, parallel to torture. Meanwhile, "who is responsible" expands with the state's "due diligence" obligation to protect its citizens from domestic abuse by private parties.

At the same time, transnational networks, global institutions such as the WHO, and modernizing states mobilized against gender violence as a threat to public health, security, and development – and the interdependent social and economic rights. After extensive testing of drivers of international conflict, Hudson and her colleagues concluded: "The very best predictor of a state's peacefulness is its level of violence against women" (2011: 205). Gender equity and women's security are linked to every aspect of economic development (World Bank 2012). Women beaten by their partners are much more likely to become infected with HIV/AIDS (UN 2008).

While, at the beginning, rape was variously denied or seen as a crime, a personal tragedy, or a humanitarian problem, a generation of feminism established sexual violence as a violation of human rights and a war crime. This has resulted in the establishment of several United Nations special campaigns – such as the UN Action Against Sexual Violence in Conflict (Stop Rape Now campaign) and a UN Special Rapporteur on Sexual Violence in Conflict. After landmark prosecutions for wartime rape at the International Criminal Tribunals for the Former Yugoslavia and for Rwanda, accountability for sexual violence in conflict expanded dramatically at the turn of the millennium with the incorporation of rape as a war crime in the statute of the International Criminal Court. The ICC recognizes rape and forced pregnancy as crimes against humanity with universal jurisdiction. The frame of rape as a war crime has continued to diffuse at the national and regional levels. Colombia's post-conflict truth commission includes an accounting for sexual violence. In 2016, Guatemala saw landmark convictions of former military officers for rape, murder, and sexual enslavement of indigenous women during the 1982 civil war.

At the global level, there are at least thirty-six UN entities with specific mandates or programs to address multiple forms of violence against women, most prominently UN Women, the UN Population Fund, UNDP, UNHCR, UNICEF, the WHO, the ILO, UNAIDS, and the UN Office on Drugs and Crime. The special agency UN Women now holds over $300 million in assets and coordinates initiatives to end violence against women in eighty-five countries. Notable among these are a *Handbook for National Action Plans on Violence against Women*, a *Handbook for Legislation on Violence against Women*, and the global program Safe Cities Free of Violence Against Women and Girls, which facilitates women's rights-based development and urban planning. Some recent examples of impact at the country level on gender violence policy by UN Women and its predecessor UNIFEM are the adoption of laws against domestic and sexual violence in Colombia,

Sierra Leone, Vietnam, and Zimbabwe, as well as police training and women's participation in Rwanda, Liberia, Cambodia, and Bosnia. UN Women also administers the separate UN Trust Fund to End Violence Against Women, which is supported by contributions from rights-promoting states. The UN Trust Fund has distributed $103 million to 393 initiatives in 136 countries and territories, and by the mid-2010s it supported eighty-six programs annually with a value of over $55 million. Another core element of the regime is the Special Rapporteur on Violence against Women at the UN Office of the High Commissioner for Human Rights (OHCHR), who is empowered to inspect country conditions, file country reports, and make recommendations that may provide leverage to multilateral and bilateral relations.

At the regional level, the Americas have serious problems – but also strong performance on reckoning with gender violence. The 1994 OAS Inter-American Convention on the Prevention, Punishment, and Eradication of Violence Against Women is remarkable in that it precedes UN norms and is a legally binding instrument for states parties, not merely a declaration. The convention has catalyzed vast improvements in data collection by many parties and the adoption of comprehensive legislation by half a dozen Latin American states. Nine countries in the region have developed national action plans mandating programs and offices on violence against women. Brazil, Colombia, Costa Rica, the Dominican Republic, Mexico, Panama, Paraguay, and Uruguay reported that they made use of the Convention of Belém in court sentencing (OAS and Council of Europe 2014).

Regional reforms have also been influential in Europe. The capstone of the European regime is the 2011 Istanbul Council of Europe Convention on preventing and combating violence against women and domestic violence. It requires states parties to pass legislative measures, ensure compliance by state actors, and use "due diligence" to prevent, investigate, punish and provide reparation for acts perpetrated by non-state actors – in their territory, by one of their nationals (with transnational reach), or by a person habitually residing in their territory (which has special relevance for migrant women). This represents a major advance in "who is responsible." Moreover, the treaty specifies states' obligation to provide legal aid for victims and gender-based asylum and to participate in a monitoring mechanism (a Group of Experts elected by a Committee of Parties). The Daphne program, initiated in 1997, is the signature EU capacity-building and grassroots funding initiative for implementation; by 2013 it was supporting almost 600 projects with a five-year budget over €100 million (Montoya 2013).

In North America, the US State Department's Human Rights and Trafficking in Persons reports, USAID evaluations, and country studies provide systematic monitoring of some forms of violence against women worldwide. At home, the US Violence Against Women Act mandates extensive monitoring, programming, and prosecution. There are potential sanctions for human trafficking and incentives for attention to gender violence in rule of law, development, and security funds. In 2013, it is estimated that State Department and USAID funds dedicated to gender-based violence totaled over $147 million. For example, between 2000 and 2009, the State Department Bureau of Population, Refugees, and Migration provided over $60 million for gender-based violence programs among Afghan refugees in Pakistan, the Rohingya in Bangladesh, and displaced women in Colombia, while the disaster relief Bureau for Democracy, Conflict and Humanitarian Assistance dedicated $7.5 million for fourteen gender-based violence protection programs in eight countries. The global Office to Monitor and Combat Trafficking in Persons spent $85.3 million on anti-trafficking assistance in 2010. At the same time, the US granted over 18,000 special protection visas for trafficking victims and their family members allowing them to remain in the country. The US fund for women and girls of the Office of Global Women's Issues hosts 116 active grants to support grassroots groups in fifty-seven countries (Siskin and Sun Wyler 2013).

The expansion of the political process to combat violence against women extends beyond global norms and programs to public policy and development initiatives with a gender- and rights-based orientation. The UN Safe Cities programs, gender-friendly transportation alternatives, the Safe Schools movement, and access to sanitation initiatives represent new mechanisms to secure women's rights to public space and participation. These initiatives reshape the human rights regime: the interdependence between security and socioeconomic rights, the growing gap between the state's "responsibility to protect" and local governance capacity. Thus, in 2010, the United Nations declared a human right to water and sanitation (UN General Assembly, A/Res/64/292, 2010) – with specific reference to the CEDAW and women's right to water (see United Nations n.d.). Since 2003, eighteen UN agencies have participated in an Interagency Task Force on Gender and Water, which has been integrated with the Millennium Development Goal process. The World Bank Program on Water and Sanitation has prepared reports and proposed initiatives on Mainstreaming Gender in Water and Sanitation (2010). In 1996, UN Habitat launched the Safer Cities Program, which now works in seventy-seven cities in twenty-four countries. Headquartered in Nairobi, the program has been especially active in Africa (with additional strength in Latin America) and has adopted a gender component; its 2012–13 report, *The State of Women in Cities*, was dedicated to women's security. The program provides monitoring, expertise, and resources for strengthening local authorities, alternative policing, urban safety audits, and grassroots participation in urban planning.

The UN Women's Global Database on Violence Against Women records seventy-two separate initiatives since 2008 to train police on domestic violence – about half in Europe and around one-third in the Americas. In Eastern Europe and Central Asia, police training on gender violence has been provided most commonly in the context of post-conflict, anti-trafficking, and rule of law programs by the UN, the EU, and the OSCE – prominently in Bosnia, Serbia, Armenia, Georgia, and Kyrgyzstan (SEESAC 2015). In the Americas, both gender violence and rule of law capacity-building have been a priority area for USAID, with additional emphasis on US assistance for domestic violence in the 2008 Mérida Initiative in Mesoamerica and the 2011 disaster assistance to Haiti. The Inter-American Development Bank has sponsored police training in Suriname and the English Caribbean, the UN Latin American Institute for the Prevention of Crime and the Treatment of Offenders (ILANUD) provided new police manuals in Honduras, and the German Organization for Technical Cooperation (GTZ) has worked with police academies in Nicaragua.

Trickling down to the national level, the "due diligence" doctrine of state responsibility for systematic violence by private actors has reshaped domestic violence policy in numerous European and Latin American states. Brazil's path-breaking 2006 Maria da Penha Law and associated programs of hotlines, shelters, and women's police was shaped by a key Inter-American Court ruling holding the Brazilian state responsible, along with a decade of women's rights mobilization. In parallel cases, the European Court held Hungary and later Turkey responsible for failure to provide effective protection of women from domestic violence, resulting in policy changes in several European states. By 2006, the UN Special Rapporteur on Violence Against Women declared this principle of due diligence established as customary international law.

In tandem, a series of Latin American mobilizations and international conferences established the frame of "femicide" to comprehend the massive unresolved public killing of women, often in a context of migration and a criminal or post-conflict crisis. Following the binational pressure on

Mexico to investigate the disappearance or serial murder of hundreds of women in the borderlands since the 1990s, by the 2000s movements against femicide produced a cascade of legislation, monitoring, new government agencies and initiatives, and investigations in dozens of Latin American countries.

At the transnational grassroots, women's movements and coalitions harness media and information politics alongside traditional protest repertoires for accountability. In India and Brazil, viral videos and Twitter campaigns complement massive street protest on sexual violence, resulting in changes in legislation, programs, and social attitudes. From Mexico to Egypt, women publicize shocking patterns of abuse, post "Harassmap" reports, secure international assistance for urban safety programs, and march to press for government response.

This expansion of information politics for women is emblematic of similar patterns of information empowerment for ethnic, religious, and sexual minorities worldwide. In the twenty-first century, "use your words" becomes "use your web." While media are not magic, the Internet can be a force multiplier for previously isolated, unrepresented, and stigmatized groups to make claims and build networks (Tufekci 2017).

Expanding Democracy: at Home and Abroad

Another dimension of expanding rights is that of extending the political process of democracy – within states and in the wider world – to address the citizenship gap. Rights are expanding at the global and transnational level, but also within states – and some states are instantiating new rights or pioneering new pathways. Although democracy is beleaguered in the twenty-first century, as we will discuss in the next chapter, some liberal democracies are incorporating more second-class citizens and keeping faith with universal institutions. While state-based promotion or "stewardship" is no longer sufficient in a multilateral and globalizing world, it is still necessary, and evolving models of state promotion can be part of the human rights ecology solution (Hafner-Burton 2013; Rodríguez-Garavito 2014).

In the worldwide panorama of potential state promoters of human rights, historic social democracies in Northern Europe, Canada, New Zealand, and Costa Rica are sometimes joined by second-wave democracies and middle-income regional powers which still benefit from universalism and seek to bolster global governance (Brysk 2009). Survivors of dictatorships in Spain, Korea, and Argentina are international promoters of the rule of law, while survivors of economic crisis, as in Brazil and the European PIGS (Portugal, Ireland, Greece, and Spain), often seek to support or extend social rights. Many among this second set of countries have also transcended a history of internal conflict to seek a more multicultural accommodation of globalization. Spain, for example, describes this rising ethos in a foreign policy document campaigning for a renewed term on the UN Human Rights Council: "We will remain faithful to our nature as a country at the crossroads between North and South, East and West – a plural, open country with a spirit of solidarity" (MAEC 2016).

Growing good Samaritans: the case of Spain

Despite economic and security challenges, Spain is a case of a newer democracy maintaining a high level of liberal democracy and "punching above its weight" in expanding norms and mechanisms for second-class citizens, non-citizens, and social rights. At home, the country provides full civil and political rights, physical security, and core social guarantees for most of its citizens most of the time (although economic crisis has eroded health care and housing). While gender violence is endemic, it is generally prosecuted, met with progressive legislation and social services, and increasingly socially sanctioned. Although monitoring groups and citizens' organizations cite problems with a new public security law limiting protest, periodic maltreatment of migrants by police, and overly broad anti-terrorism legislation and incommunicado detention, these issues are episodic rather than systemic – and the government does respond to domestic complaints and the recommendations of international bodies. To wit, Spain has undertaken two Universal Periodic Reviews for human rights performance under the UN peer review mechanism, working with its strong ombudsman office, and has responded to 169 of the international body's 189 recommendations (a typical rate of findings for a developed democracy).

On the international front, Spain has served on the United Nations' Human Rights Council from 2013 and is currently seeking another term, citing its strong treaty commitments – including extensions of individual complaint optional protocols and the service of Spanish experts to global institutions – and foreign policy priorities. It has been active throughout the international system in campaigning for the abolition of the death penalty; an end to discrimination by gender and sexual orientation; disability rights; the human rights to safe drinking water and sanitation; and increased control of business and human rights. During Spain's presidency of the UN Security Council in 2015, it promoted the passage of a landmark resolution on Women, Peace and Security (2242). Despite economic austerity, Spain supports a special major international fund for access to clean water (MAEC 2016). In overall aid, the country provides a high level of meaningful international cooperation with special emphasis on social rights and marginalized groups, and in 2017 it allocated over €250,000 to international organizations promoting peace and human rights. In international law, for at least a generation, Spanish jurisprudence has contributed notably to universal jurisdiction for torture and forced disappearance, beginning with the Pinochet case against the former dictator of Chile and extending to a series of Latin American cases.

Despite a conservative Catholic cultural history, Spain has been a world leader in expanding rights for its LGBT citizens. Emerging from a devastating civil war and almost forty years of fascist dictatorship in 1975, within a generation it had prohibited discrimination by sexual orientation or gender identity and recognized domestic partnerships. In 2005, Spain was in the earliest wave of countries to legalize same-sex marriage, as well as full adoption rights for same-sex couples. Gays serve openly in the military, transgender reassignment is readily registered, and homophobic harassment is rare. The country offers immigrants asylum on the basis of persecution by gender, sexual orientation, and gender identity.

Spain has also advanced the treatment of Europe's most marginalized minority group – the Roma, with an estimated population over 1 million – the largest in Europe. Although Roma still experience inequities in social conditions and have suffered from austerity cuts, Spain provides them with better recognition of their social rights and access to justice than any of its European neighbors. Over the past decade, it has established the following governmental responses: the National Council on the Gitano Population (2005), the Council for the Promotion of Equality and Non-Discrimination based on Racial Origin or Ethnicity (2007), and a "Plan of Action for Gitano Development 2010–2012" (FSG 2012). The development plan for improving education, access to the labor market, housing, and social inclusion was assessed by the leading NGO, Fundación Secretariado Gitano (FSG), as slow but successful. Following national efforts in the European context, in 2012 Spain launched a longer-term Roma Framework with the European Commission under the EU initiative for National Roma Integration Strategies up to 2020. The European Commission evaluated the country's record as "promising," including educational measures to foster school completion, a national Roma health survey, and regional housing programs in Andalusia and Catalonia (European Commission 2014).

While Spain exceeds the declining European norm in refugee protection, in this area an ethos of expansion has defaulted to a lower-level conservation of fundamental standards. Faced with far fewer arrivals than its Mediterranean neighbors, Spain has maintained reasonable processing and accommodation conditions for most asylum seekers on Iberian territory. Moreover, Spanish civil society is so supportive that there have been repeated demonstrations demanding that the Spanish government accept *more* refugees (Al Jazeera 2017b). In 2016, Spain offered some form of protection to about half of 16,000 asylum seekers, but there are delays and shortfalls (The Local 2017).

The broader range of African and Middle Eastern migrants to Spain are reported to suffer some discrimination and police harassment, as well as exclusion from some social rights – notably, under austerity cuts, health care is no longer provided to migrants. Spain has been a transit and destination zone for both labor and sex trafficking, especially from Nigeria, Romania, and China. Of the roughly 1,000 cases identified each year, about two-thirds involve women, and most of these have been sexually exploited. In response, Spain adopted legislation in 2010 and an ombudsman program in 2011. There have been several recent prosecutions of Nigerian gangs in Barcelona and, previously, of Chinese labor traffickers (US Department of State 2015).

Conditions are even worse for asylum seekers from Ceuta and Melilla, Spain's enclaves adjacent to Morocco, who have been detained under harsh conditions, at times physically harassed, and at times deported to danger. Spain has attempted to improve compliance with its international obligations by agreeing to accept additional refugees from the UN and within the EU, but implementation has been greatly delayed. The agreement in 2016 to take almost 1,500 additional refugees from the Middle East has, as of fall 2017, reached around only 300 Syrians, while Spain's commitment to protect over 17,000 from Italy and Greece has resulted in around 1,300 relocations. With a population of around 45 million and massive unemployment, Spain's commitment to this level of resettlement and attempt to maintain access to asylum is laudable, but clearly in this regard its reach exceeds its grasp.

Hope for the Future?

We have tracked an important movement of expansion of rights agendas, voices, and mechanisms that have the potential to improve some of the gaps in the rights regime. These are dynamic and cumulative, and in some cases provide potential transferable models for broadening the reach and deepening the meaning of human rights.

But, at the same time, there is another movement towards contracting rights. In some cases, changing conditions stress long-standing gaps beyond repair. In others, there are new and worrisome articulations of nationalism, hierarchy, and dehumanization. We turn now to analyze this counter-movement of contraction and its relationship with the growth and preservation of the international human rights regime.

4

Contracting Rights:
Regression and Resistance

In the fall of 2016, I returned to an America that frightened me. There were hate crimes on my campus, and some of my students feared deportation. My academic networks buzzed with urgent action alerts: Hungarian authorities tried to shut down the Central European University – where I had been invited to lecture on human rights just the year before. Turkish colleagues with whom I had toasted the spread of freedom at international conferences were fired, banned, arrested. After mere months in Trump's America, my friends and family were dispirited by the daily outrage to civil liberties, social justice, safety, truth – and simple human decency. But, by that winter, we remembered how to respond. The day of the LA Women's March, by the time my car reached the outskirts of the city, the crowds had grown so much that Los Angeles shut down its metro system for the first time. When we finally arrived, standing beside my students, neighbors, and a rainbow of strangers, texting coast-to-coast with three generations of my family all marching in their cities, we began to reclaim our democracy. I saw Jewish and Muslim women marching together in solidarity against religious prejudice, a huge Planned Parenthood contingent defending women's health and freedoms, signs for the Black Lives Matter movement against police violence, and a migrant rights banner claiming inclusion: "You can't spell America without Maria." The ultimate sign of the times – which inspired this book – was the one that read: "It's not a moment, it's a movement."

The third movement of human rights is contraction, reinforcing gaps and contrasting with expansion – but constantly met with contestation. The contraction of human rights represents both a shrinking of "who is human" in the face of the rising responsibilities profiled in the last chapter and a retreat from regime responsibilities. In this sense, it is more than a lag or a breakdown of the long-standing system as outlined in chapter 2. Another worrisome feature of declining rights is regression in "what is right" in state policy, public opinion, and international doctrine. Established civil rights are attacked with counter-frames of security, exclusionary nationalism, and patriarchal tradition that position freedom as a threat to identity and safety. Solidarity shrinks with the claim that minority rights compete with the collective rights of majorities. Twenty-first-century human rights resistance involves an active movement to counter illiberal states and populist publics shrinking the public sphere through dehumanization and deinstitutionalization.

States and populist political parties contest cosmopolitanism with claims that institutional globalization of governance threatens the social rights and the well-being of national majorities. The combination of two other forms of negative globalization is the context shaping rights regression claims: neo-liberal economic globalization and transnational terror. Twenty-first-century economic globalization shifts the liberal social compact, the impact of linkage, and material interdependence, sparking a retreat from global legal institutionalization, from Brexit to withdrawal from the ICC. Epic levels of inequality shape a defensive rise of chauvinistic nationalism and religious fundamentalism – as the only available forms of solidarity. Meanwhile, securitization takes hold in response to transnational terror, as a genuine rise in external threat is filtered through the promotion of moral panic by nationalist and military elites to inspire backlash. An ironic tragedy of rights contraction is that worried publics afflicted by negative forms of globalization are manipulated by elites to reject the global rights regime that represents their best hope of countering their collapsing citizenship.

The overlapping forms of contraction span states, societies, international relations, and citizen attitudes. First, human rights contract with the rise of illiberal regimes that curtail the rights of their own citizens and adopt foreign policies that undermine international rights institutions. At another level, states, political parties, and communities mobilize backlash in rights norms that may result in the unchecked persecution of previously protected or ignored outsiders – whether migrants or marginalized citizens. At the same time, a trend towards militarization and the privatization of state security functions – even in democracies – allows decision-makers to evade accountability for protection and due process. Finally, there is a global deflation of rights norms in favor of rival beliefs and contested international affiliations.

The effects of this contraction complex contribute to rights gaps; they also check expansion and create new problematics which the system is not designed to contemplate. The security gap widens with resilient assertions of sovereignty and deflections of citizenship. Expanding global governance mechanisms and processes falter in the face of the rise of illiberal powers and interstate constituencies. Old and new claims and voices struggle to register in a Zeitgeist marked by shame fatigue and resurgent parochialism.

The contraction of rights manifests in regression in illiberal states, in dehumanizing backlash movements, and in counter-cosmopolitanism at the global level. We will consider the pattern and impact of each facet of rights resistance below: deflating democracy in Turkey, homophobic regression in

Uganda and Chechnya, and retreat from international rights institutions. At the same time, a salutary difference between newer contractions of rights and long-standing gaps is that contemporary regressions are quickly contested by a more extensive repertoire constructed from prior waves of struggle. We will see the reconstruction of resistance at the national level that may provide an emerging platform for the next wave of rights movement. Finally, we will explore the full range of nationalist backlash, isolationist retreat, and resurgent resistance in an extended treatment of the contemporary US.

Rights Regression

The rise of democracy worldwide has been blunted by stalled transitions, regressions, and illiberal regimes that undermine civil liberties in their treatment of minorities and dissidents. Beyond behavioral non-compliance typical of the security gap, both states and local civil societies may regress and reject hard-won international norms – reversing expansions of citizenship and standards of "what is right" – especially in areas of high perceived threat such as national insecurity and struggles over sexual and religious identity. Unlike historic authoritarianism, these deflated democracies generally retain some mechanisms of majority rule and popular participation but decouple minority rights, civil liberties, and the rule of law.

In most of these reactionary cases of contraction, it is fear of rights that drives new wrongs, as the successful development of new rights norms and policies at home and those proposed internationally trigger counter-mobilization and state suppression. Deflating democracies may ban, attack, or condition international and local human rights monitors and defenders. Alas, the international regime offers little recourse against state violence, censorship, harassment, or defunding of rights defenders or rising second-class citizens.

The pattern of deflating democracy is epitomized in Turkey but is also characteristic of Russia, Hungary, Venezuela, India, Israel, and the Philippines, among others. Russia represents a post-authoritarian petro-populism, similar to Venezuela and several Central Asian states. Civil liberties and public protests are systematically suppressed, NGOs are banned, journalists and dissidents are assassinated, and LGBT citizens are persecuted. Requirements that human rights organizations register as "foreign agents," online surveillance, and patriarchal legislation repressing women and sexual minorities are mechanisms of rights suppression that have diffused to other illiberal regimes. Russia has also diminished human rights in the wider world through its annexation of Crimea, its support for Assad's war crimes in Syria, and its opposition to international institutions, including the UN Human Rights Council (Human Rights Watch 2017).

In Hungary, a similar post-communist suppression of civil society is combined with right-wing nativist party control. Particular features of Hungary's rights regression are the persecution of Roma, violent detention of refugees, and measures targeting academic freedom and international universities. Poland, Greece, and Finland have also seen significant electoral gains by far-right anti-immigrant political parties that have advocated punitive policing and border control, religious and ethnic intolerance, and various levels of patriarchal "traditional values" resulting in threats to reproductive and sexual minority rights – but also pushback by national forces. Similar but more modernized nativist parties achieved unexpected regional and parliamentary presence in Austria, the Netherlands, and France, but were ultimately spurned in national elections in favor of centrist coalitions.

India and Israel present distinct yet convergent patterns of democratic distortion as ethno-majoritarian governments influenced by religious fundamentalist parties suppress and discriminate against minorities, commit war crimes in occupied conflict zones, and ultimately diminish civil liberties for dissenting elements of the dominant population. In Israel, Palestinians are systematically denied citizenship and social rights, due process and access to justice, and freedoms of movement and assembly and are subject to police abuse and vigilantism. Israel's Adalah Legal Center for Arab Minority Rights lists over fifty discriminatory laws that systematically disadvantage Arab citizens on the basis of religion and origin (Adalah 2016). War crimes in occupied areas include the collective punishment of civilians, attacks on medical facilities, the use of prohibited weapons, illegitimate detention, and inhumane treatment. But, recently, the conflict has begun to spill over even further – into derogation of democracy for Israel's majority Jewish population. As in India, Israel now hosts military censorship of journalists, prohibitions on NGOs and registration of foreign funding, government restrictions on the speech of human rights groups in schools and military institutions, a new government "Ethics Board" vetting the political content of the educational curriculum, and arrests for peaceful protest by majority Jewish Israelis questioning policies towards Palestinians (Shafir 2018).

Deflating democracy: the case of Turkey

After almost a century of top-down modernization and liberalization, by the turn of the millennium Turkey was considered a peripheral European polity and a model for "Islamic democracy." However, the rise of the Islamic populist Erdoğan government brought a decline in civil liberties, an increase in ethnic discrimination, regression in women's rights, and an anti-democratic use of counter-terror legislation to prosecute civil society advocates and human rights defenders (Amnesty International 2015b; BBC News 2017b). Kurdish citizens have been especially affected, and even majority Turks who support Kurdish rights or speak out against discrimination have been sanctioned for such acts as signing a peace petition. One of Turkey's most prominent authors, Orhan Pamuk, was jailed for discussing the Armenian genocide as such.

Following a murky coup attempt in 2016, the Erdoğan government systematically targeted democratic institutions and civil society, dismissing over 100,000 judges, lawyers, professors, and civil servants, arresting tens of thousands, and banning thousands of NGOs and social service organizations associated with opposition movements. Even those fired but not jailed face additional loss of passports, state pensions, and housing, together with threats by public officials that regularly result in harassment and violence. In June 2017, for example, Turkey arrested the head of that country's Amnesty International on ill-founded and inconsistent charges of support for the Gulenist coup sponsors – based on "evidence" such as his use of a messaging application also used by some members of now-banned civic organizations.

Additional path-breaking breaches in the rule of law by the Turkish regime include political persecution of democratic opposition office-holders. The arrest of a whistle-blowing opposition party MP, who was subsequently sentenced to twenty-five years in prison, for exposing illicit Turkish intelligence service collaboration with Syrian armed groups generated massive public protest. At the same time, in the summer of 2017, a prominent Turkish judge who served as an official of the UN's Mechanism for International Criminal Tribunals was convicted of "membership in a terrorist organization." This repressive counter-cosmopolitan move breached international relations norms of diplomatic immunity, and Turkey went on to defy an order of release from the UN body that is legally binding on the country under its international status in the global organization (BBC News 2017a). In another international spillover of Turkish repression, Turkish embassy security forces violently attacked peaceful protesters in Washington, DC, and blocked local police from protecting American citizens, creating a diplomatic incident (Hermann 2017).

Contesting Regressions

Many of these alt-authoritarian regressions have been met with more international condemnation and domestic protest than transpired in earlier eras of dictatorships. In India, for example, a group of prominent writers have refused government prizes to delegitimize the Hindu party government's discriminatory failure to prosecute fundamentalist and communal violence, such as lynching of beef-eating Muslims and dissident Hindu scholars. After the latest lynching in 2017, a protest campaign, "Not in my Name," rallied thousands across India, with a strong presence of youth (Wire Staff 2017). International academic networks, the European Commission, and a broad spectrum of national civil society have mounted vigorous protests against Hungary's persecution of the Central European University. Mass protests recur in Turkey despite threats, arrests, and censorship: there have been significant demonstrations following Erdoğan's internationally challenged April 2017 referendum expanding his executive powers and the arrests of opposition figures profiled above, as well as protests contesting military abuses in Kurdish areas. In a symbolic march of 450 kilometers from Ankara to Istanbul, hundreds of thousands of Turkish defenders of democracy carried banners saying "adalet" (justice) and garnered massive support (Shaheen and Hatunoğlu 2017; Gall 2017). In Russia, thousands of opposition supporters, minority rights advocates, and Russian legal advocacy movements have challenged a range of restrictions of civil liberties in Russia's own Constitutional Court as well as in the European system. They recently secured a judgment from the European Court ruling against Russia's discriminatory law forbidding "gay propaganda" (Rankin 2017). We will examine below one of the most concerted movements of resistance in the deflating democracy of the US, alongside the decline of the US as a hegemonic promoter of global institutions.

Counter-Cosmopolitanism

Meanwhile, rights are contracting at the global and interstate level as well as regressing within declining democracies. A combination of illiberal trends in leading powers, post-colonial nationalism, and diffuse backlash against the liberal modern world order conspire to undermine cosmopolitan norms and institutions.

Among the dominant states, the narrative of right-wing populism combines the appeal to an authentic movement of legitimate citizens against an unresponsive political elite, an ethnocentric majority identified with traditional values allied against "outsiders," and a strategic use of an oppositional stance against dominant cultural norms to channel anger from the real or perceived displacement of globalization (Greven 2016). This is the logic that explains the alt-right's anti-modern, nationalist, patriarchal ideology, which bears a family resemblance to fascism but may differ in features such as economic model and mode of military influence. Such counter-cosmopolitan forces are gaining traction in the US, the UK, and Australia, as well as in European right-wing political parties.

Beyond the West, in the aftermath of empire – including the Soviet and Chinese spheres of influence – emerging states struggle to establish political stability and coherent social hierarchies in a neo-liberal world with turbulent globalizing, urbanizing societies. Reinvention of traditions of religious fundamentalism and hyper-nationalism offer solidarity and justify the position of political elites in Africa, Southeast Asia, Eastern Europe, Central Asia, and the Middle East. While in a previous generation, young democracies in Latin America were eager to lock in global governance that empowered globalizing middle classes, twenty-first-century transitional and post-conflict societies revert to leadership by ethnic, dominant-party, dynastic, and resource cliques that benefit from localizing power relations. This configuration of power is also counter-cosmopolitan.

At the transnational level, globalizing trade, migration, education, and modernizing social roles have not produced widespread empowerment – and instead have displaced some dominant citizens from long-standing social rights and status, opening a new front in the citizenship gap. At the same time, the promise of cosmopolitanism heightens a sense of relative deprivation, as the modest success of expanding rights has improved the potential claims of some formerly marginal groups even as dominant groups decline. Normative resistance to rights results from a backlash against the perception of a failed social contract of cosmopolitanism that instead produces a citizenship "race to the bottom." It is telling that twenty-first-century populists and isolationists dehumanize, securitize, or relativize perceived competitors and claims rather than rejecting the concept of rights itself. They no longer argue against "what is right" – instead, they counter-claim that certain people are not really human members of the rights-bearing community, that their presence or claims are too dangerous, or that their rights threaten the majority or some collective rights such as religion. Therefore, an appropriate response is not simple promotion of rights, but advocacy for interdependence.

Dehumanization: the case of homophobia

In an era of a spreading tipping point for rights protection of sexual orientation and gender identity, an anti-LGBT backlash has appeared from a variety of disparate standpoints. Even as post-colonial regimes in the global South decry cosmopolitan norms of diversity as a Western contradiction of non-Western local traditions, the religious right in Russia, Eastern Europe, and the US condemns gay rights precisely as an affront to Western Christian civilization. Sexual orientation and gender identity (SOGI) rights and individuals are under assault in most of Africa, South Asia, and the Middle East, as well as in Russia and its neighbors. Although Catholicism has historically stigmatized homosexuality, a number of contemporary Catholic countries in Europe and even in Latin America have adopted progressive policies on same-sex marriage, hate crimes, and discrimination. The fault lines of homophobia, in countries that are also often regressive on women's rights, appear to reflect a reinvention of tradition to scapegoat identities that represent imagined subversions of patriarchal nationalism in the face of national crisis and collapsing citizenship. For example, Russia's persecution of gays is matched by a downgrading of its domestic violence law to allow physical abuse that does not leave permanent injury, with the explicit justification of promoting "family values."

Anti-gay backlash against universal norms of non-discrimination spans the gamut of oppositional identities. In Uganda, Christians claimed that tolerance of gay rights threatened African cultural traditions. But the Ugandan religious groups were highly influenced by American missionaries who visited the country in 2009 – months before anti-gay legislation with a death penalty was drafted – ironically reflecting the imposition of a rival fundamentalist universalism rather than a defense of an indigenous identity. Uganda is an underdeveloped and ethnically fractured country that suffered the bloody dictatorship of Idi Amin in the last generation and, more recently, a fierce civil war with cultish northern rebels that displaced a large population. The current administration of President Museveni is conservative, neo-liberal, and pro-Western; it famously advocated education in abstinence for epic rates of HIV/AIDS rather than proven public health measures such as the distribution of condoms. In 2014, at the urging of Christian groups and in opposition to the growing Westernization of gender roles, the Ugandan Parliament passed an anti-homosexuality law mandating potential life imprisonment and requiring citizens to report suspected homosexuals. Although, since draconian measures were initially vetted (in 2009), the regime had suffered US criticism, suspension of World Bank loans, and aid cuts from the Netherlands,

Norway, and Denmark, the ongoing anti-gay campaign gained wide public support and was used by the government to "make anti-gay sentiment synonymous with patriotism." The government blamed an "international gay lobby" for promoting homosexuality in Uganda, local newspapers published threatening lists of supposed gays, and harassment and exile became a common experience for SOGI Ugandans. During the run-up to the bill, a prominent gay activist was murdered (D. H. 2014).

Chechnya presents a different syndrome of chronic political violence, personalist authoritarianism, tribal nationalism in the Caucasus, and oppositional Islam but with similar homophobic results. In 2017, when Russian-linked gay rights groups applied for pride parade permits against a background of rising patriarchal policies and religious influence, the Chechen government launched a "preventative" crackdown on gays. In what survivors labeled a "pogrom," hundreds of men were beaten, threatened, detained, and tortured. Several were killed or released to families who were urged to commit "honor killings." A local network has smuggled victims out of the country, amid worldwide protest. The leader of Chechnya denies the campaign, affirmed by Human Rights Watch – because he denies that there are gays in Chechnya (Kramer 2017). European leaders, such as Chancellor Angela Merkel of Germany, urged Chechnya's dominant power, Russia, to restrain the abuses, to no avail. Instead, Russian LGBT activists protesting the Chechen persecution were themselves arrested by Russian authorities (Barber 2017).

As in Russia itself, and most of the homophobic backlash countries, persecution of gays is embedded in a larger patriarchal regression that also affects women's rights:

> Under the unconditional patronage of Russian President Vladimir Putin, Kadyrov rules his republic as a totalitarian, and has done so since taking power in May 2004, after his father, then President Akhmad Kadyrov, was assassinated.

Years before the campaign against gays, his commandos launched a similar crackdown on "badly behaved" women. The bodies of 13 women were found in different parts of the republic. The women had been tortured and then shot in the head. These murders were the subject of human rights activist and journalist Natalia Estemirova's last investigation before she herself was abducted and killed in August 2009. (Taimienova 2017)

Crossing from rights norms to global governance, in the second and third generation of globalization of law, the designated human rights institutions still fail to overcome the constraints of state sovereignty – and some members even come to question the foundations of universalism. Globalization in general, and global institutions in particular, have failed to deliver for broad global publics. The liberal progenitors of the post-war international order have become illiberal, isolationist, or both. Regression in the rights regime combines long-standing failures of compliance with more fundamental rejection of the authority or legitimacy of international institutions.

Regression in the rights regime

We can track the rejection of the rights regime across every facet of global governance. At the global level, anti-democratic powers such as Russia, China, and Saudi Arabia stand on sovereignty to block UN Security Council, Human Rights Council, and treaty body condemnation of even the most egregious abuses. At the same time, these very regimes bankroll war crimes in Syria and Yemen, genocide in Sudan, and resource-based dictatorships throughout Africa. Pariah states disable the mechanisms designed to contain them: they cripple broadly based treaties such as CEDAW with reservations, eschew optional protocols to norms such as the International Covenant on Civil and Political Rights that permit standing by civic actors or international monitoring, or block monitoring visits. In a telling reflection on decades of experience as an international law scholar and UN Special Rapporteur, Philip Alston chronicles new modes of rejection of global monitoring in Mauritania, China, and the Human Rights Council itself (Alston 2017). At the same time, the liberal founding fathers of the global institutions are in retreat. The US has been a veritable "deadbeat dad" of the UN system for almost a generation, refusing to support global liberal undertakings it proposed, drafted, or previously collaborated with the Western bloc to underwrite, from the CEDAW treaty to the International Criminal Court. Recently, the US has cut essential financial contributions to the UN as a whole and the UN Population Fund in particular, equivocated on the Human Rights Council, retreated from diplomatic coordination with the human rights treaty bodies and Special Rapporteurs, and even announced that US foreign policy will no longer systematically consider human rights conditionality, which had sometimes operated to complement UN sanctions. In the face of a spate of terror attacks, the British Prime Minister Theresa May similarly lashed out against human rights and European norms as an impediment to security. While Anglo-American liberal internationalism has always coexisted with rights-abusive foreign relations, especially in wartime and post-colonial relations, recent withdrawals rob a fragile world order of a productive stock of hypocrisy – "the tribute vice pays to virtue" (Blakeley 2009).

International courts are suffering systematic deconstruction. A set of African states have withdrawn from the International Criminal Court, and there is rising resistance to its exercise of the defining power of prosecution of sitting heads of state (Ainley 2018). The most powerful regional body, the European Court, has suffered increasing nonadherence to judgments (Sandholtz 2018) – with unclear consequences from Brexit and the rise of Euroskeptic movements in key European states. The Inter-American Human Rights Court, another key regional institution that had been gaining traction in the troubled continent, suffers extreme backlogs and has become so severely underfunded that its investigatory commission was almost shuttered in 2016.

Regime Resilience

Yet, even here, a reformed global order is emerging. Germany, Canada, and France have declared their independence from US foreign policy, with specific reference to refugees, among other issues. The Netherlands and Canada have offered funds targeted to women's reproductive rights organizations to replace US aid cuts and UN Population Fund defunding. South Africa has now reversed its withdrawal from the ICC. In 2017, Australia agreed to pay over $35 million compensation to almost 2,000 asylum seekers detained in Manus under inhumane conditions and now plans to close the facility, reversing a long-standing practice widely criticized by the UN and international refugee advocacy groups (Al Jazeera 2017a).

Exception or vanguard: which way USA?

The current state of human rights in the United States illustrates the competing trends of contraction: rights regression and resilience, counter-cosmopolitanism and contestation. The 2016 election of Donald Trump has been both a catalyst for a current wave of contracting rights and the culmination of a longer-term rising tide of illiberalism and isolationism. Trump's disdain for democratic institutions in favor of populist affirmation and the mobilization of followers to violence achieve unprecedented levels, involving elements of fascism. However, his counter-cosmopolitan hyper-nationalism and racist and xenophobic rhetoric and policy proposals are heightened articulations of recurrent themes in American politics that are also increasingly shared by Anglophone allies and the European right. In a strange irony, Trump's explicit call for American exceptionalism ("make America great again") is no longer exceptional, reflecting a global trend of anti-global hegemonic decline. While the full fascist complex is typically associated with rising powers, democratic regression and the scapegoating of minorities and migrants is also characteristic of the end-stage of empires. As Steve Bannon, the president's key ideologue and former White House advisor, put it, "This whole movement has a certain global aspect to it," linking Trump's rise to a constellation of populist revolts across Europe. "People want more control of their country. They're very proud of their countries. They want borders. They want sovereignty. It's not just a thing that's happening in any one geographic space" (Tharoor 2016).

Historically, the US is a muddled mix of a flagship liberal democracy built on slavery and conquest, with exemplary levels of freedoms and almost non-existent social rights. American exceptionalism has manifested in foreign policy with a similarly schizophrenic combination of democracy and rights promotion alongside a systematic refusal of international accountability and an episodic retreat to isolationism (Forsythe and McMahon 2016). Worse, the US as a hegemon has directly sponsored or indirectly authorized war crimes, torture, and political repression worldwide – from the Vietnam War to the Pinochet dictatorship, from Guantánamo to Gaza. The sovereignty gap and citizenship gap combine in areas such as a racially discriminatory death penalty, retained by the US alone among its peers. Yet the security gap has been attenuated for most Americans during most periods, and strong judicial autonomy and a vigorous civil society have combined to check – in the long run – some of the most egregious systemic abuses, such as the Jim Crow version of American apartheid.

For several generations, human rights in the US have begun to expand in some directions parallel to worldwide trends. Formerly second-class citizens such as women and ethnic minorities gained significant new rights through the protection of voting rights, federal anti-discrimination legislation, affirmative action in education, and civic movements. New forms of rights such as same-sex marriage and environmental justice have traction in the coastal states inhabited by a majority of Americans. Decades after their European peers, American civic movements' claims to social rights such as housing, water, and health care have begun to gain legitimacy – and, in the latter case, the American Health Care Act was established as the first national social security program since the New Deal.

Yet the Trump agenda represents an attack on every element of "who is human, what is right, and who is responsible." Trump's dehumanizing stigmatization of Mexican migrants and attempt to ban Muslims from entering the US represent a shocking regression in American political discourse, unimaginable as recently as 2015. His administration's attempts to roll back health care, the protection of civil liberties, freedom of information, and women's reproductive rights amount to a systematic dismantling of "what is right." Meanwhile, a shrinking regulatory structure and a decline in diplomacy, along with the decentralization and privatization of state coercive institutions, diminish "who is responsible" for rights protection. In Trump's America, significant sectors of the population face systematic threats to life, liberty, and equality.

Dehumanizing and violent discourse by Trump and his allies has been associated with a rise in harassment and hate crimes against immigrants and religious and ethnic minorities in the US. There have been thousands of incidents of violence and harassment reported, including dozens of arson attacks and several bias-inspired murders of Muslim, South Asian, black and Latino Americans. In emblematic incidents, the *New York Times* reported: "A black college student was fatally stabbed in College Park, Md., days before he would have graduated. Two men were killed and another wounded when they tried to stop a man's hateful rant on a train in Portland, Ore." Islamic Americans also report hundreds of cases of discrimination by law enforcement officials, around half connected to new exclusionary immigration policies (North 2017). This parallels the upsurge in attacks in the UK following the Brexit vote (ProPublica 2016). The assassination of a peaceful protester, Heather Heyer, by a neo-Nazi terrorist in Charlottesville, Virginia, in 2017 – inexcusably excused by President Trump – demonstrates that racist violence has spilled over to affect the routine exercise of civil rights by the privileged majority population.

In the other facet of rights regression as the culmination of long-term trends associated more with the security state than the populist president, the US has passed the threshold of a "deadly democracy." Capping a long-standing pattern, police shot and killed over 900 Americans in 2016 and 461 in the first half of 2017. About half of those killed were black or Latino (Washington Post 2017). Black citizens are about three times as likely as whites to be shot by the police. The vast majority of police are never even charged for shootings of unarmed civilians, and, of the few dozen who are, a mere handful have been convicted of wrongdoing (Park 2017). Further diminishing accountability, Trump's Attorney General, Jeff Sessions, has suspended the consent decrees mandating federal monitoring and reform of police departments judged to show a pattern of abuse and violations of constitutional rights. A fresh development of impunity in 2017 was Trump's presidential pardon of the Arizona Sheriff Joe Arpaio, who had been convicted of massive violation of the civil rights of Latinos both by racial profiling them as potential immigrants and by their unwarranted, abusive, protracted detention in sub-standard facilities.

In another chronic failure of rights currently assuming new dimensions, the US has the world's highest incarceration rate. There are over 2 million Americans in prison or jail – at least one in five for a non-violent drug offense. Due process of law is biased by race and class, as discriminatory policing, prosecution, fines, and bail processes, along with a dearth of public defenders, result in a systematic lack of access to justice. Thus, African-Americans, who form 13 percent of the US population, make up 39 percent of those incarcerated (Wagner and Rabuy 2017). Prison conditions are inhumane; overcrowding, violence, lack of health care, and abuse of solitary confinement have generated numerous judgments against American prisons – with only limited amelioration (such as California's *Plata v. Brown* and Arizona's *Parsons v. Ryan*). After decades of debate on failed drug policies and the social cost of mandatory sentencing, bipartisan prison reform proposals emerged in the waning years of the Obama administration – but Attorney General Sessions has opposed these reforms and revived maximal drug prosecutions. Even worse, he blocked an Obama initiative to phase down sub-contracting to for-profit prisons, which had been charged with extensive abuses (see Shapiro 2011).

At ground zero of the citizenship gap, migrants are affected by a combination of discrimination, detention, and lack of due process – and as with citizens, rising patterns of abuse have reached new heights under Trump's policies. Over 40,000 migrants are detained by Immigration and Citizenship Enforcement (ICE) in a mix of local and private prisons. An additional 16,000 convicted solely of immigration crimes such as border-crossing are now housed in federal prisons, which consist mostly of a separate system of thirteen criminal alien facilities run by private companies (Wagner and Rabuy 2017). An investigation by the American Civil Liberties Union in 2014 of the five private federal immigration prisons in Texas documents abusive isolation, overcrowding, lack of medical treatment, and forced labor (ACLU 2014). As part of Trump's January 2017 executive order on immigration, 10,000 additional personnel will be hired to patrol the border – and more immigration prisons will be constructed to detain and subsequently deport undocumented migrants. In April 2017, Trump approved a new $110 million construction in Texas, to be run by one of the private companies that has been repeatedly sued for abuses (Aguilar 2017).

Although the detention of migrants and the number of forcible deportations and workplace raids had risen under the Obama administration, Trump has rolled back exceptions carved out for deferred action for undocumented childhood arrivals (so-called Dreamers – referring to the American Dream of welcoming immigrants). Trump also reversed the Obama-era limitation of immigration enforcement to concentrate on undocumented migrants charged with a criminal offense and broadened collateral detention of family members. In the winter and spring of 2017, ICE conducted vastly increased raids in Texas, California, and New York that detained thousands of people – in some cases, formerly protected undocumented migrants identified during warranted searches of homes and workplaces for accused criminal aliens. Furthermore, asylum seekers picked up in 2017 (mainly women and children from Central America) have been subject to detention and in some cases summary deportation without full hearings or access to representation. In several cases, migrants were detained from courthouses where they were seeking protection from criminal abuse – in at least one instance, a woman was detained as she was seeking an order of protection as a victim of domestic violence. The Trump administration has especially targeted dozens of "sanctuary cities" that shelter migrants from federal prosecution and has attempted to enforce blanket ICE orders by state and local authorities in a number of other regions which routinely report only criminally charged aliens. Even in Texas, concerned local officials and law enforcement are resisting this collaboration as a violation of civil rights and a barrier to public safety (Flynn 2017).

Perhaps the apogee of rights regression in Trump's America has been the self-denominated "Muslim ban" mandating a suspension of immigration arrivals from seven majority-Muslim countries, including previously approved visa-holders and refugees. Trump's executive order also called for an unclear program of potentially discriminatory "extreme vetting" (which overlapped in certain regards with existing refugee screening procedures). Although the order was ruled unconstitutional, then redrafted but legally blocked in its revised version, and is now partially restored pending appeal, it was initially enforced in a discriminatory fashion that denied due process to thousands of persons. When the initial order came into force, travelers arriving from the designated countries were detained at US airports and questioned by ICE and Transportation Security Administration officials; some were returned, accepted refugees and visa-holders in transit were stranded and refused carriage by airlines, and families were separated. After chaotic days of protest and legal appeals, the initial order was blocked as religious discrimination, and many of its initial victims were released – but some had lost their refugee status, visas, jobs, scholarships, or family reunification and some remain barred from legal entry to the US. The revised order was enforced more briefly and systematically, avoiding the spectacle of airport detentions of tearful toddlers and confused grandmothers in the name of national security, but it nevertheless blocked due process and the consideration of refugee status for a number of asylum seekers. Both episodes appear to have produced some cases of refoulement – the return of refugees to danger in Iraq and Afghanistan – including of applicants for asylum who had been endangered by their work with American military forces during the conflicts in those countries.

For citizens and migrants alike, burgeoning efforts to ensure equal rights in voting, education, and the workplace for all Americans have also been attacked or dismantled by the Trump administration. At the direction of Attorney General Sessions, the Justice Department has dropped claims against discriminatory voter ID laws in Texas and federal guidelines on school discrimination for sexual orientation or gender identity. President Trump directly blocked an

Obama order that had mandated federal contractors' compliance with anti-discrimination provisions in the workplace. The Trump administration Labor Department has dropped numerous investigations and, under its proposed 2018 budget, will dissolve its discrimination complaint office. The Education Department under Betsy DeVos has drastically cut back its Office of Discrimination and level of investigation. Even the Environmental Protection Administration has been ordered to shut down its Environmental Justice program, which examines the impact of pollution on minority communities and offers some assistance (Eilperin et al. 2017).

Last but not least, Trump's open endorsement of dictators and rollback of human rights foreign policy has arguably contributed to the plight of victims of abuse worldwide. Although US human rights conditionality has always been inconsistent and often ineffective, American diplomacy has played a positive role in some key moments over the past generation – and is credited by human rights advocates in some countries with protecting them. However, Secretary of State Rex Tillerson announced that the US would no longer consider human rights in aid or alliances. From his election onwards, Trump has granted preferential treatment to leading dictators and expressed support for their repressive policies. He increased aid to Egypt's General al-Sisi even as he shuttered NGOs and tortured political prisoners. Trump hosted Philippine President Duterte, infamous for bragging of the extrajudicial execution of thousands of drug suspects – not to mention his recent encouragement to soldiers in a militarized zone fighting rebels to rape "up to three women," stating that he himself would take legal responsibility. Trump granted new weapons to Saudi Arabia, despite its own political repression and abuses of women's rights, as well as sponsorship of war crimes in Yemen (Rucker 2017). Responding to a journalist's challenge regarding Trump's enthusiasm for the Russian leader Vladimir Putin, who has presided over a crackdown on dissidents and journalists, Trump excused the alliance with the cynical and unconcerned relativism that the US itself had committed rights abuses (Pengelly 2017).

#Resist

Yet the US now stands at the vanguard of resistance as well as regression. Some liberal democratic institutions and America's vaunted civil society are contesting each contraction, holding the line on "what is right" and "who is human," even though they have less leverage over "who is responsible." Hundreds of thousands of Americans have mobilized to protest, petition, and campaign for racial justice, women's rights, fair migration, freedom of information, and health rights in an unprecedented loose coalition of Resist movements (Holland 2017). There have been vocal and pluralistic Black Lives Matter protests around dozens of recent police shootings and verdicts. The January 2017 Women's Marches in dozens of cities formed the largest mass protest in US history, attracting millions – with 750,000 participants in Los Angeles alone – and have been followed by Marches for Science and Climate Justice. The Indivisible movement of former political staffers has organized well-attended congressional district town hall events throughout the US to spotlight and discredit Trump's attempt to repeal Obama's health care system, which would have removed health insurance from over 20 million Americans. In the aftermath of Trump's moral equivocation on neo-Nazi violence in Charlottesville, the CEOs of major corporations resigned from his business advisory councils, the entire Presidential Arts Commission disbanded, and several diplomats stepped aside.

Although immigrants' rights have been historically more controversial, the outrage of the Muslim ban caused both a surge of Americans protesting at every major airport where travelers were detained and a special movement of hundreds of volunteer lawyers, who spontaneously converged to represent them and have formed an ongoing support service. The flagship legal advocacy group the American Civil Liberties Union saw its membership and donations grow exponentially following the election of Trump – and it is this organization that mounted the first successful legal challenge to the Muslim ban, along with contesting other discriminatory measures such as voting rights restrictions and, more recently, the proposed ban on military service by transgender individuals. Americans have even mobilized to protect undocumented migrants, notably the childhood arrivals who have labeled themselves "Dreamers." There is a strong solidarity movement for this population called United We Dream, many universities offer sanctuary to undocumented students, and legal defense networks and faith-based support have flourished for undocumented migrants affected by aggressive enforcement and family separation.

American institutions have also shown some resilience in defending the rule of law against populist caprice. Both iterations of the Muslim ban were quickly blocked by a series of district courts; subsequently, a further-curtailed version limited to "foreigners with no claim of relationship to the US" in six countries was allowed to operate temporarily pending review by the Supreme Court in fall 2017. Several key regions have declared their independence from Trump's immigration enforcement, including the states of Connecticut, California, Massachusetts and Washington, as well as the major cities of Chicago, Miami, and New York. The day after the election, the governor and the state legislature of California passed resolutions affirming the civil rights of all Californians under the state constitution, which grants greater protection than the national constitution in several areas, including free speech, criminal justice, and gender equity. California has also passed legislation banning state-funded travel to other states with discriminatory legislation – currently applied to half a dozen Southern states with limitations on public services or religious exemptions to deny private services by sexual orientation. Several recent high court decisions have struck down racially discriminatory restrictions or documentation requirements of voting rights in North Carolina, Alabama, Georgia, and Kansas. During the confirmation hearings for Attorney General Sessions, an exchange between the Republican Senate majority leader Mitch McConnell and Democratic Senator Elizabeth Warren came to embody both the decline and the defense of American democracy. Because Sessions had a controversial record opposing civil rights, Senator Warren sought to introduce historic testimonial into the congressional record: condemnation of Sessions's regression by the civil rights leader Coretta Scott King – the widow of slain African-American advocate Martin Luther King. But the new Republican majority under Trump sought to restrict civil rights, not only through appointments and policy proposals but through curtailing transparency, debate, and free speech. In this case, McConnell used his parliamentary position to attempt to quash Warren's intervention – and, when she demurred, he imposed censure and cut her off. He famously justified his action: "She was warned, she was given an explanation. Nevertheless, she persisted."

But Warren's persistent defense of civil rights, free speech, and women's rights became a rallying cry for protest and political organizing to resist the Trump agenda. And it is an appropriate conclusion to the future of human rights as movement.

Think Globally, Act Nationally?

In the wake of worldwide contractions and counter-cosmopolitanism, some advocate a re-emphasis on national-level reinforcement of the human rights regime (Brysk 2017b). National-level movements may mobilize successfully for global norms horizontally within a citizenship frame – for example, in India the "right to food" campaign – while other campaigns may assume a national character or local repertoires as they translate and reinterpret global rights beyond the global regime (Hertel 2017; Engle Merry 2006). Rights reform may circulate at a subnational level and even across regions (O'Brien 2013). A particularly powerful growing form of localization is the emergence of "human rights cities": dozens of urban governments that have adopted human rights standards for direct local implementation (Oomen et al. 2016). Another domesticating movement of human rights is to relink interdependent civil-political and economic-social rights struggles to recover the global social democratic ethos of solidarity that inspired the rights revolution – for example, in the right to health (Rodríguez-Garavito 2016).

The moral of the movement contesting contraction falls under two principles listed in the introductory chapter: "stick together" and "keep moving." Despite dozens of declining democracies, civic resistance and global solidarity have checked abuses on the ground, from Uganda to the United States. The cosmopolitan institutions and ethos of the international human rights regime have struggled to reinvent rights globally in a post-liberal, renationalizing era. Yet the social capital and evolving strategies of rights as a movement continue to grow. We turn now to the future of that project: reconstructing rights.

5

Reconstructing Rights in a Post-Liberal World

At this crossroads of movements, what can the study of human rights tell us? Alone, we struggle with the contradictions of history, the indeterminacy of social science, and assaults from many quarters on the "dream of a common language" and public sphere. But, together, the community of human rights scholars can discern patterns and pathways to guide our efforts. The movements I have outlined in this book draw upon a series of edited volumes I have convened over the past decade, each incorporating roughly a dozen scholars' voices: Globalization and Human Rights, People Out of Place, The Politics of the Globalization of Law, Expanding Human Rights, *and* Contracting Human Rights. *Over the past year, I have attended a more recent wave of workshops and conferences with scores more scholars to assess the state of human rights worldwide. We agree that we are witnessing fundamental changes in the global order and that the rights regime must respond – but we do not agree on why or how. To close our inquiry, I will attempt to project some of the scenarios sketched by the community of scholars to strategies for the rights regime, movement, and ethos. What we can offer are not answers but better ways to ask the right questions and better tools to understand the way the world works – so that we can shape it within our powers.*

We have seen that human rights is at the same time a movement for social change, an emerging mode of global governance, and an ethos of mediation between norms and power. Human rights are above all a persistent representation of three core social questions: "Who is human?" "What is right?" and "Who is responsible?" As we have traced the movement of human rights into the twenty-first century and towards the future, rights are at the same time lagging, expanding, contracting – and contesting. Understanding the drivers, patterns, and relationship of these movements is the best way to construct a meaningful response.

As we have discussed, rights are lagging on account of the security gap and the citizenship gap – rooted in a contradictory combination of persisting sovereignty and collapsing governance. Increasing drivers of human insecurity in the twenty-first century include contemporary forms of conflict that evade accountability, the declining protection of physical integrity in democracies, and surging numbers of "people out of place." While there has been an expansion of human rights norms and mechanisms to reach different levels of global governance and different facets of the human condition, these have gone further to reach second-class citizens and to deepen transnationalism than to address distorted fundamentals of state repression and armed conflict.

Meanwhile, rights are contracting through the decline of domestic and international institutions, illiberal hegemony, and the rise of counter-norms of patriarchal nationalism and fundamentalism. These challenges and regressions reflect the shifting structural conditions of neo-liberal inequality and the threat to transnational security, but they operate in dialectical tension with the heritage of generations of rights struggles, sticky institutions, and resurgent mobilization. Moreover, the diffusion and translation of rights movements to new geographic and social terrain contest these attempts to shrink "who is human," continue to expand notions of "what is right," but struggle to gain accountability for "who is responsible" under changing governance relations.

We can affirm that human rights remain the last best hope of the global order through their power to transform governance through expanding voice, claims, and tools. However, although human rights remain necessary, the historic rights regime will not prove sufficient. The critics are correct that some claims of human rights are exaggerated and collapsing – but that does not mean that the good, grounded work won by generations of struggle should be abandoned; rather, reform is necessary. Human rights do not equal and cannot automatically produce justice; but rights are the guarantee of a fair and open space to seek justice. And the pursuit of a just society and world under changing social conditions is the difference between life and death, now more than ever.

Constructing the Future

Given these trends, what can we see as options for the future? Our discussion thus far suggests that the way forward lies in expanding regime coordination, addressing gaps in citizenship, building institutional capacity in law and public policy, bridging social-democratic rights interdependence, working horizontal global governance channels, and crafting new vocabularies of grounded universalism. The potential for each of these reforms will depend on the interaction of the global trend and the national or issue-specific dynamic which we can model below.

For the global trend, a recent leading collective analysis of the futures of human rights outlines several alternative scenarios and strategies for human rights: *staying the course*, *pragmatic partnership*, *global welfarism*, and *sideshow* (Hopgood et al. 2017). These alternatives correspond to reinforcing the existing human rights regime, reforming the regime to incorporate different sets of states and constituencies, extending rights systematically to social welfare and economic justice issues, and setting aside rights struggles in favor of other rubrics for mobilization. In the terms presented for the movements in this book, these alternatives would map onto policy predictions:

- staying the course to develop the current international regime to repair the *gaps*;
- pragmatic partnerships and global welfarism by *expanding* movements, mechanisms, and social rights norms; or
- the decline of human rights into a sideshow through counter-cosmopolitan *contraction*.

But, as we have seen in this analysis, these are simultaneous movements – and they are all contested.

And, in addition to the global scenarios, we must add national-level struggles, as international relations scholars track a "two-level game" for rights. In this book, we have considered four illustrative national models:

1 *collapsing in the gap*: failing states, armed conflict, and people out of place (Mexico);
2 *expanding*: transnational networks, issue interdependence, rights promoters (Spain);
3 *declining*: populism, fundamentalism, illiberal powers (Turkey); and
4 *contesting* contraction: liberal legacies, civic movements (US).

Therefore, the pathway to reform must be tailored to the possible future. Staying the course may help expand rights in a solid citizenship regime, but global welfarism will be critical to counter illiberal populism. Pragmatic partnerships will be useful for interdependent rights promotion in democratic, developing, and even declining states – but will not be sufficient in failing states, armed conflict, and acute citizenship gaps.

Once we have identified the genre of change that is appropriate, we must consider further the strategies and tactics that produce human rights reform. In the next section, we will profile the historic pathways of change charted by human rights scholarship, consider what has changed, and connect them to the types of problems each might address. We will then turn to the final task of considering how to rise to the challenge – layer by layer – through repairing the regime, mobilizing the movement, and rethinking the cosmopolitan ethos.

The Crisis of Cosmopolitanism: Pathways of Change

Global governance and cosmopolitan commitments are in transition in the twenty-first century with shifting parameters of political economy, security, and ideology, but aspects of the international human rights regime can adapt – and even lead. For two generations, the ensemble of international human rights institutions and mobilizations has appeared to gain traction – at least in some places and times. But now, despite increases in the numbers of people reached by democratic freedoms, some kinds of social rights, and transnational accountability, the worldwide refugee crisis, impunity for massive war crimes, the rise in xenophobia and discrimination, and deteriorations in civil liberties in democratic and authoritarian regimes alike bespeak a decline in the regime itself – not just lingering gaps in enforcement. Currently, we face a crisis of cosmopolitanism – the architecture, ethos, and practice of multilateral universalism – in which the efficacy and even the legitimacy of global governance are increasingly called into question. The good news is that international regimes are interactive and adaptive, so that changes and challenges in one area may compensate in another – and a tailored response may be effective even when the regime as a whole has declined. The first step is to analyze how the human rights regime worked, when it worked, and whether those pathways of change still function – or how to repair them. Human rights scholarship on effectiveness and compliance outlines the main dynamics of how transnational human rights pressure works: *interdependence, diffusion, legalization, framing,* and *shaming.* In an era of widespread democratization, access to information, and mobilization in social capital, *domestication,* and citizenship may also be a parallel pathway that was not envisaged in the original regime. While international institutions may be central to interdependence, diffusion, legalization, and framing, global civil society is also critical for diffusion, framing, and shaming. Improving effectiveness requires analyzing the potential of, barriers to, and changes in these pathways.

The first human rights regime pathways to assess are the material and institutional forces that shape all international relations. First, states – and transnational actors such as corporations or development banks – may respond to human rights claims because they are enmeshed in international accountability through relationships of "moral and material" *interdependence* that renders them vulnerable to pressure (Risse et al. 2013), such as economic sanctions or valuable membership in international organizations (Brysk 2009). Second, international institutions and practices may circulate and *diffuse* to the local level with powerful effects (Sikkink 2011; Greenhill 2015; O'Brien 2013). Globalizing the *rule of law* generally fosters greater human rights compliance, although only under certain conditions (Brysk 2013a). These structural forces often work even better together when they cross international and national levels. There are increasing findings of supportive interactions between commitment to international human rights norms, grassroots pressure, and strengthening domestic legal and democratic institutions (Simmons 2009; Sandholtz 2017; Stobb 2015).

Alongside material pressures and law, rights gain influence through the power of communication introducing new and effective voices, frames, expertise, and performances of human rights claims that resonate with an audience. Communication is a highly interactive pathway that works at multiple levels and is generally associated with human rights movements and campaigns (Brysk 2013b). Different rights *frames* shape new regime repertoires, as labeling an abuse may produce treaties, committees, and Special Rapporteurs that increase recognition and spill over to policy options. Some frames – for example, genocide – legitimate intervention, carry dedicated resources from the international community, or tap into the foreign policy of particular promoter states. Creating new frames such as "femicide" can generate grassroots mobilization, national legislation, and the diffusion of state responsiveness.

Another kind of leverage for norms may come through the oldest and most widespread international tactic of *naming and shaming*. Cross-national studies establish that "citizens will perceive the human rights conditions in their country more negatively when their country is shamed by the international community" (Ausderan 2014). Historically, some studies trace how naming and shaming have been effective to advance human rights during democratic transitions, while others show how states respond to castigation by Amnesty International combined with treaties, even in non-democracies (Hawkins 2002; Clark 2001). But, like legalization and interdependence, clearly this form of influence works only under certain conditions – and it appears that those conditions are changing.

What has changed in these pathways of influence? How do the shifts in the overall parameters of globalization translate into changes in the dynamics of rights – and how can the international human rights regime respond? On the downside, twenty-first-century economic globalization does shift the impact of linkage and material *interdependence* in a way that diminishes response to aid conditionality and sanctions. The rise of emerging economies which are often illiberal and exceptionalist as trade partners and investors – for instance, China – subverts some of the leverage of cosmopolitan institutions. On the normative side, *naming and shaming* has also suffered deflation and exhaustion through linkage with a beleaguered cosmopolitan ethos and the conscious promotion of nationalist counter-norms that replace shame with pride in rights violations justified by honor or identity. The power of *framing* contends now with the mobilization of a new wave of national security counter-frames (Brysk and Stohl 2018).

However, the decline of liberalism and the rise of nationalism has less impact on *diffusion* and *framing*. Both horizontal *diffusion* of law and policy models and multi-level transnational mobilization around evolving *frames* are more resilient than interstate and national human rights regimes. *Framing* remains a potent strategy for humanitarian and socioeconomic issues even when civil-political rights are challenged. And, at the national level, some countries *domesticate* some kinds of rights through various combinations of expanding citizenship, translating international norms into local vocabularies, and mobilizing horizontal movements and coalitions.

To recover effectiveness, the human rights regime must respond to these shifts through strategic analysis of the record and logic of expanding rights, repairing gaps, and resisting contraction. What, then, are the reform possibilities within and beyond the current rights regime to harness these changes? Some possible configurations are outlined in table 5.1.

Even within a limited reiteration of the current rights regime ("stay the course"), there is scope for ameliorating rights gaps with rights promotion capacity-building that fosters autonomous and rights-based *legal institutions*, unbundled from democracy. And, in the spaces available for

Table 5.1   Rights-constructing strategies

	Gaps	Expanding	Contracting	Contesting
Stay the course	Unbundle democracy	Broaden citizenship	Increase functional ties	Use information politics
Partnership	Domesticate rights	Increase access	Translate rights to local	Build solidarity networks
Social welfare	Build capacity	Bridge norms	Rights-based public policy	Forge indivisibility
Sideshow barriers	**Impunity**	**Hierarchy**	**Deflation**	**Displacement**

expanding rights, extensions of *citizenship* establish political resources for future empowerment, mobilization, and state incentives to attend to the claims of newly included members. The rights regime has also shifted governance leverage through increasing recognition of the *functional interdependence* between law and other facets of public policy such as urban planning or water, along with rights-based development, health, and environment networks (as we saw with indigenous peoples). In the most limited scenario, *information politics* still has some traction to contest contraction.

Further, we can move to strategies of diversifying the human rights regime's partnerships and broadening its scope to more systematic social rights to recover the social welfare agenda. This leads to an expanded menu of options for the regime. Even in areas of gaps, social rights partnerships seem amenable to *domestication*. In zones of contraction, social rights may still be available for *translation* into local rubrics of solidarity – for example, more liberal forms of nationalism that include social rights and try to expand their reach. The human right to water is a strong illustration of this trend (Baer 2017). Even as material interdependence morphs in unhelpful directions, moral and institutional interdependence can be fostered by *horizontal* and transnational human rights forums and programs. In some areas, despite gaps and contractions, social rights and some aspects of physical security can progress through *capacity-building* and rights-based *public policy* rather than law – such as urban planning for women's safety.

From this framework, we can plot more specific strategies for the international regime, rights campaigns, and development of the rights ethos.

Repairing the Rights Regime

What can the international organizations of the rights regime do if we see them as a form of media rather than authority (Brysk 2009)? Information politics is still at the heart of what the human rights regime does, and it still matters – but the shifting efficacy of the pathways of influence changes how and why it matters. While signaling for sanctions matters less, the diffusion of norms, mechanisms, repertoires, and expertise still matter greatly in some areas. Moreover, as interstate institutions, treaty bodies may sometimes secure better access to information through site visits or even partial or inaccurate government reports than their non-governmental counterparts – and we should analyze and take advantage of this division of labor. Information politics has always played broader roles in the regime that go beyond naming and shaming. Reporting mechanisms produce patterned data, grant voice and standing to civil society, help foster networks of expertise and advocacy, and assist in building new frames. Recent research suggests that even government self-reporting contributes to state socialization, bureaucratic capacity, and circulation of information to domestic challengers (Creamer and Simmons 2016).

International bodies serve as an arena for *voice*, above all the voice of non-citizens and second-class citizens that lack recognition as well as rights at home – refugees, indigenous peoples, domestic workers. International recognition can help break domestic denial, mobilize transnational constituencies, and sometimes coordinate common programs for border-crossing problems such as human trafficking. Global institutions help build, bridge, and expand rights *frames* – through norm declaration but also through production of reports, conferences, and exchanges. International forums can argue for and demonstrate the normative and functional *interdependence* of rights in areas such as health, which increases their intersectional reach at the same time as it broadens their appeal. Finally, rights bodies can use their promotional and educational functions to *translate* the cosmopolitan ethos to more inclusive, participatory forms, from publicizing hidden histories to peer exchanges on the meaning of rights in diverse social contexts.

The international regime must reform and invest in these areas, including access and standing for civil society and advocates, horizontal and parallel forums, convoking expertise on rights interdependence, and fostering rights promotion dialogues. Beyond naming and shaming, in the next generation we should emphasize rights framing and claiming. Along with that exercise, global institutions should become a space to reflect on their own pathways of influence through studies of best practices and consciously to innovate, to domesticate – and, at times, simply to persist.

Mobilizing the Movement: Constructing Global Citizenship

The global process of mobilization must become more targeted to appropriate repertoires and frames for different types of violations, national problematics of gaps or contractions, and international opportunity structure. "Using the right tool for the job" is more important – and more complicated – than ever. Those tools may be multi-level and multi-directional, no longer relying on either top-down or "boomerang" effects in a patterned sequence from above and below (Keck and Sikkink 1998). Often, human rights campaigns will need to think globally and act nationally. As state and interstate governance shifts, the global civic toolbox of standard-setting, strategic litigation, seeking sanctions, and consciousness-raising must often be supplemented by civil society acting directly to provide services, build capacity, participate in public policy, and organize human rights education.

We have seen how the future of human rights mobilization embodies the facets laid out in the introduction: words, money, and collective action. In a shifting environment, "use your *words*" matters in different ways. Voice is essential for humanizing the citizenship gap, presenting counter-norms to illiberal nationalism and fundamentalisms, framing patterns of abuse, and socializing publics to new and evolving roles as global citizens. The essential messages to global publics and policy-makers are empathy and interdependence, and human rights campaigns are positioned to speak these truths of common connection and humanity to power.

At the turn of the millennium, human rights campaigns learned to "follow the *money*" in broadening governance from authority to market relations. Enhanced human rights conditionality or promotion moved further from the modes of trade, aid, and investment sanctions to labor standards, boycotts, fair trade, social responsibility in production and investment, and social enterprise. After expanding the economic means of human rights, human rights as a movement must now expand the economic ends, refocusing on the interdependence of social justice with civil and political rights. Campaigns and translation of social rights between *indivisible* economic rights and physical security are the foundation of the future of rights – and, indeed, of global governance.

The future of human rights also depends on the reconstruction of community. We have seen that *solidarity* provides the basis for expansion of rights access and mechanisms, while *indivisibility* of the rights of various sectors is the most sustainable response to contraction. This means that rights mobilizations must always attend to vulnerabilities of race, class, gender, and other forms of identity and social position – but build common rather than competitive understandings and claims of historic disadvantage. While collective rights can and should be extended for marginalized groups such as indigenous peoples, group rights cannot substitute for the democratic pathway to self-determination and may exclude people with mixed, multiple, or transnational identities. Building rights-based coalitions across national and transnational communities is perhaps the most urgent and lagging task of the human rights movement.

Finally, rights campaigns must *keep moving*. New forms of power, ideologies, and media require constant evolution of rights rhetoric and repertoires. Although the efficacy of mobilization ebbs and flows, the waves of resistance are cumulative, laying down new layers of consciousness and habits of collaboration with each tide.

Human Rights as Ethos: a Post-Liberal Humanism?

In the twenty-first century, it now appears that the social contract of liberalism as a world order is in crisis – but it can be reconstituted on new terms. The presence of new voices in an enlarged public sphere can adapt "rights talk" via the translation of global norms into vernacular concepts and repertoires to build local support. At the same time, it is critical to restore recognition of common human dignity across lines of conflict and manipulation.

In some form, the underlying values of a pragmatist humanism precede and parallel the Western Enlightenment basis of modernity and will survive the waning of Western hegemony. Historic sources of universalism and human dignity range across cultures, from medieval Jewish and Islamic humanists to Confucian proponents of the rule of law, from indigenous peoples' notions of cosmic unity and intergenerational responsibility to the African *umbuntu* ethic of care. The subset of human rights that are individual legal entitlements of freedoms as claims against the modern state are indeed intertwined with liberal social contracts and interstate compacts. But even these notions are being rearticulated in Latin American and African constitutions incorporating multicultural and social rights, transnational movement claims for reproductive and environmental justice, and expanded ideas of citizenship, including global and local as well as national participation rights. Unfolding global dialogues are building globalized understandings of rights – especially for migrants, minorities, and intergenerational justice.

Building on these global and historic elements, a post-liberal humanism is possible. While an expanded ethos must incorporate and fortify humanitarian protection and legal defense, it must move beyond to multidimensional empowerment: political, economic, and cultural. We are already moving rights talk from fostering autonomy to creating capacity, from fear to hope, and from individual emancipation to enabling social conditions. Now, we must extend a consciousness of rights to every aspect of our social life as a human community – and our presence on a shrinking planet.

Such an ethos must present an affirmative defense against competitive notions and counter-norms, constantly demonstrating the cost of a human rights "race to the bottom." An ironic consequence of the global challenges of the twenty-first century is the linkage of vulnerabilities across political and cultural boundaries, from epidemic diseases to climate-driven forced displacement. Positive modeling and socialization can show that together we rise, raising awareness of the virtuous cycles of cooperation to solve the inescapable common problems of the human condition, starting with state power but moving far beyond.

The future of human rights is a movement towards expanding our response to the questions – and articulating these expanding answers in practices of mobilization and solidarity constructs the future we need and deserve. We do "make our own history, although under conditions not of our choosing" (Marx 1852).

- Who is human?
  - *Everyone* – citizens and strangers, capable and needy, worthy and despicable.
- What is right?
  - *Freedom, equity, and dignity* – growing in relation to shifting forms of power.
- Who is responsible?
  - *All sources of authority* – global institutions, the community of nations, national governments, transnational corporations, civil society organizations, local communities, families, and individuals; as civil servants, soldiers, voters, workers, consumers, employers, and neighbors.

The future of human rights is not fixed, but we can chart its movement and shape its motion – because the future of human rights is in our hands.

References

ACLU (American Civil Liberties Union) (2014) *Warehoused and Forgotten: Immigrants Trapped in Our Shadow Private Prison System*. New York: ACLU.

Adalah (2016) Discriminatory Laws in Israel, www.adalah.org/en/law/index.

Aguilar, Julian (2017) White House Greenlights a New Immigration-Detention Center in Texas, *Texas Tribune*, 14 April.

Ainley, Kirsten (2018) Retreat or Retrenchment? An Analysis of the International Criminal Court's Failure to Prosecute Presidents, in *Contracting Human Rights: Crisis, Accountability, and Opportunity*, ed. Alison Brysk and Michael Stohl. Northampton, MA: Edward Elgar.

Al Jazeera (2017a) Australia to Pay $53m to Manus Island Asylum Seekers, 14 June, www.aljazeera.com/news/2017/06/australia-pay-53m-manus-island-asylum-seekers-170614054721385.html.

——— (2017b) Madrid Protesters Demand Spain Take in More Refugees, 17 June, www.aljazeera.com/news/2017/06/madrid-protesters-demand-spain-refugees-170617203137700.html.

Alston, Philip (2017) The Populist Challenge to Human Rights, *Journal of Human Rights Practice* 9(1): 1–15.

Amnesty International (2015a) *Report 2014/15: The State of the World's Human Rights*, www.amnesty.org/download/Documents/POL1000012015ENGLISH.PDF.

——— (2015b) Amnesty on Turkey's Worsening Human Rights Record: 11 Key Issues, https://humanrightsturkey.org/2015/02/24/amnesty-on-turkeys-worsening-human-rights-record-11-key-issues/.

Anaya, Alejandro, and Barbara Frey, eds (forthcoming) *The Human Rights Crisis in Mexico*. Philadelphia: University of Pennsylvania Press.

Apodaca, Clair (2018) The Human Rights Costs of NGOs' Naming and Shaming Campaigns, in *Contracting Human Rights: Crisis, Accountability, and Opportunity*, ed. Alison Brysk and Michael Stohl. Northampton, MA: Edward Elgar.

Arendt, Hannah (1951) *The Origins of Totalitarianism*. New York: Harcourt, Brace.

——— (1958) *The Human Condition*. Chicago: University of Chicago Press.

Ausderan, Jacob (2014) How Naming and Shaming Affects Human Rights Perceptions in the Shamed Country, *Journal of Peace Research* 51(1): 81–95.

Baer, Madeline (2017) The Human Right to Water and Sanitation: Champions and Challengers in the Fight for New Rights, in *Expanding Human Rights: 21st Century Norms and Governance*, ed. Alison Brysk and Michael Stohl. Northampton, MA: Edward Elgar.

Barber, Laurence (2017) LGBTI Activists Arrested Protesting Torture of Gay Men in Chechnya, *Star Observer*, 2 May, www.starobserver.com.au/news/international-news-news/activists-arrested-gay-torture-chechnya/157853.

Barnett, Michael N. (2011) *Empire of Humanity: A History of Humanitarianism*. Ithaca, NY: Cornell University Press.

Batha, Emma (2016) Europe's Refugee and Migrant Crisis in 2016: in Numbers, *World Economic Forum*, 5 December, www.weforum.org/agenda/2016/12/europes-refugee-and-migrant-crisis-in-2016-in-numbers.

Baxi, Upendra (2002) *The Future of Human Rights*. Oxford: Oxford University Press.

BBC News (2017a) Turkey Jails UN Judge in "Breach of Diplomatic Immunity," 15 June, www.bbc.com/news/world-europe-40285658.

——— (2017b) Turkey Police Hold Rights Activists including Amnesty Chief, 6 July, www.bbc.com/news/world-europe-40517184.

Beitz, Charles R. (2009) *The Idea of Human Rights.* Oxford: Oxford University Press.

Blakeley, Ruth (2009) *State Terrorism and Neoliberalism.* London: Routledge.

Bonello, Deborah, and Erin Siegal McIntyre (2014) Is Rape the Price to Pay for Migrant Women Chasing the American Dream?, http://splinternews.com/is-rape-the-price-to-pay-for-migrant-women-chasing-the-1793842446.

Boyle, Alan (2012) Human Rights and the Environment: Where Next?, *European Journal of International Law* 23(3): 613–42.

Brysk, Alison (2000) *From Tribal Village to Global Village: Indian Rights and International Relations in Latin America.* Stanford, CA: Stanford University Press.

——— (2001) *Globalization and Human Rights.* Berkeley: University of California Press.

——— (2005) *Human Rights and Private Wrongs: Constructing Global Civil Society.* London: Routledge.

——— (2009) *Global Good Samaritans: Human Rights as Foreign Policy.* Oxford: Oxford University Press.

——— (2013a) *The Politics of the Globalization of Law: Getting from Rights to Justice.* London: Routledge.

——— (2013b) *Speaking Rights to Power: Constructing Political Will.* Oxford: Oxford University Press.

——— (2017a) Expanding Human Rights, in *Expanding Human Rights: 21st Century Norms and Governance*, ed. Alison Brysk and Michael Stohl. Northampton, MA: Edward Elgar.

——— (2017b) The Future of Human Rights, *Global-E*, 5 January, www.21global.ucsb.edu/global-e/january-2017/future-human-rights.

——— (forthcoming) *The Struggle to End Violence Against Women: Human Rights and the Dynamics of Change.* Oxford: Oxford University Press.

Brysk, Alison, and Gershon Shafir (2004) *People out of Place: Globalization, Human Rights, and the Citizenship Gap.* New York: Routledge.

Brysk, Alison, and Michael Stohl, eds (2017) *Expanding Human Rights: 21st Century Norms and Governance.* Northampton, MA: Edward Elgar.

———, eds (2018) *Contracting Human Rights: Crisis, Accountability, and Opportunity.* Northampton, MA: Edward Elgar.

Business and Human Rights Resource Centre (2015) Chinese Investment Overseas, 10 March, https://business-humanrights.org/en/chinese-investment-overseas.

——— (n.d.) Corporate Legal Accountability, https://business-humanrights.org/en/corporate-legal-accountability.

Cardenas, Sonia (2014) *Chains of Justice: The Global Rise of State Institutions for Human Rights*. Philadelphia: University of Pennsylvania Press.

Charlesworth, Hilary (2002) International Law: A Discipline of Crisis, *Modern Law Review* 65(3): 377–92.

Clark, Ann Marie (2001) *Diplomacy of Conscience: Amnesty International and Changing Human Rights Norms*. Princeton, NJ: Princeton University Press.

Cohen, Roger (2016) Broken Men in Paradise, *New York Times*, 9 December, www.nytimes.com/2016/12/09/opinion/sunday/australia-refugee-prisons-manus-island.html.

Cornwall, Andrea, and Celestine Nyamu-Musembi (2004) Putting the "Rights-Based Approach" to Development into Perspective, *Third World Quarterly* 25(8): 1415–37.

Creamer, Cosette D., and Beth A. Simmons (2016) *Do Self-Reporting Regimes Matter? Evidence from the Convention against Torture*, https://scholar.harvard.edu/files/cosettecreamer/files/creamersimmons_catselfreporting_feb2016.pdf.

D. H. (2014) Deadly Intolerance: Uganda's Anti-Gay Law, *The Economist*, 25 February, www.economist.com/news/middle-east-and-africa/21597943-diplomatic-pressure-did-not-stop-absurd-law-deadly-intolerance.

de Sousa Santos, Boaventura (2002) Toward a Multicultural Conception of Human Rights, in *Moral Imperialism: A Critical Anthology*, ed. Berta Hernández-Truyol. New York: New York University Press, pp. 39–60.

Doherty, Ben (2015) Children in Detention Exposed to Danger, Human Rights Commission Finds, *The Guardian*, 11 February, www.theguardian.com/australia-news/2015/feb/11/children-in-detention-scathing-criticism-in-human-rights-commission-report.

Douzinas, Costas (2000) *The End of Human Rights: Critical Legal Thought at the Turn of the Century*. Oxford: Hart.

Eilperin, Juliet, Emma Brown, and Darryl Fears (2017) Trump Administration Plans to Minimize Civil Rights Efforts in Agencies, *Washington Post*, May 29, www.washingtonpost.com/politics/

trump-administration-plans-to-minimize-civil-rights-efforts-in-agencies/2017/05/29/922fc1b2-39a7-11e7-a058-ddbb23c75d82_story.html?utm_term=.a96a44b5c92c.

Engle Merry, Sally (2006) *Human Rights and Gender Violence: Translating International Law into Local Justice*. Chicago: University of Chicago Press.

European Commission (2014) The European Union and Roma – Factsheet: Spain, http://ec.europa.eu/justice/discrimination/files/roma_country_factsheets_2014/spain_en.pdf.

European Court of Human Rights (2017) *Migrants in Detention*, www.echr.coe.int/Documents/FS_Migrants_detention_ENG.pdf.

Flynn, Meagan (2017) City Officials in Houston and across Texas Announce Plans to Sue over Sb4, *Houston Press*, 17 May, www.houstonpress.com/news/city-officials-across-texas-in-houston-mount-summer-of-resistance-and-will-sue-state-over-sb4-9445817.

Forsythe, David P. (2017) Hard Time for Human Rights, *Journal of Human Rights Practice* 16(2): 242–53.

Forsythe, David P., and Patrice McMahon (2016) *American Exceptionalism Reconsidered*. New York: Routledge.

FSG (Fundación Secretariado Gitano) (2012) *Politicas de inclusión social y población gitana en España: el modelo español de inclusión social de la población gitana*, www.gitanos.org/upload/18/83/Politicas_de_inclusion_social_y_poblacion_gitana_en_Espana__ES.pdf.

Gall, Carlotta (2017) "March for Justice" Ends in Istanbul with a Pointed Challenge to Erdogan, *New York Times*, 9 July, www.nytimes.com/2017/07/09/world/europe/turkey-march-for-justice-istanbul.html?_r=0.

Gauri, Varun, and Siri Gloppen (2012) *Human Rights Based Approaches to Development: Concepts, Evidence, and Policy*. Washington, DC: World Bank.

Gearty, Conor (2016) *On Fantasy Island: Why the Human Rights Act Matters*. Oxford: Oxford University Press.

Gogou, Kondylia (2017) The EU–Turkey Deal: Europe's Year of Shame, 20 March, www.amnesty.org/en/latest/news/2017/03/the-eu-turkey-deal-europes-year-of-shame/.

Gómez Isa, Felipe (2017) Indigenous Peoples: From Objects of Protection to Subjects of Rights, in *Expanding Human Rights: 21st Century Norms and Governance*, ed. Alison Brysk and Michael Stohl. Northampton, MA: Edward Elgar.

Goodale, Mark (2009) *Surrendering to Utopia: An Anthropology of Human Rights*. Stanford, CA: Stanford University Press.

Goodhart, Michael (2009) *Human Rights: Politics and Practice*. Oxford: Oxford University Press.

—— (2016) Human Rights as Political Tools, Paper presented at the Western Political Science Association Annual Conference, San Diego, California, March.

Greenhill, Brian (2015) *Transmitting Rights: International Organizations and the Diffusion of Human Rights Practices*. New York: Oxford University Press.

Greven, Thomas (2016) *The Rise of Right-Wing Populism in Europe and the United States*. Berlin: Friedrich Ebert Stiftung.

The Guardian (2017) *The Defenders*, www.theguardian.com/environment/series/the-defenders.

Hafner-Burton, Emilie (2013) *Making Human Rights a Reality*. Princeton, NJ: Princeton University Press.

Harcombe, Kathy (2016) Israel's Unwanted African Migrants, 3 February, www.bbc.com/news/magazine-35475403.

Hathaway, James C., and R. Alexander Neve (1997) Making International Refugee Law Relevant Again: A Proposal for Collectivized and Solution-Oriented Protection, *Harvard Human Rights Journal* 10: 115–211.

Hawkins, Darren (2002) Human Rights Norms and Networks in Authoritarian Chile, in *Restructuring World Politics: Transnational Social Movements, Networks, and Norms*, ed. Sanjeev Khagram, James V. Riker and Kathryn Sikkink. Minneapolis: University of Minnesota Press, pp. 47–70.

Healy, Claire (2015) *Targeting Vulnerabilities: The Impact of the Syrian War and Refugee Situation on Trafficking in Persons*. Vienna: International Centre for Migration Policy Development.

Hermann, Peter (2017) Turkish Guards Will Be Charged in D.C. Protests, Officials Say, *Washington Post*, 14 June, www.washingtonpost.com/local/public-safety/turkish-guards-will-be-charged-in-embassy-protests-officials-say/2017/06/14/fecee1ea-46d1-11e7-bcde-624ad94170ab_story.html?utm_term=.3d6b06208d81.

Hertel, Shareen (2017) Forging Alternative Routes to Norm Change: Economic Rights Protagonists, in *Expanding Human Rights: 21st Century Norms and Governance*, ed. Alison Brysk and Michael Stohl. Northampton, MA: Edward Elgar.

Hiskes, Richard P. (2015) *Human Dignity and the Promise of Human Rights.* New York: Open Society Foundations.

Holland, Joshua (2017) Your Guide to the Sprawling New Anti-Trump Resistance, *The Nation*, 6 February, www.thenation.com/article/your-guide-to-the-sprawling-new-anti-trump-resistance-movement/.

Hoover, Joe (2016) *Reconstructing Human Rights: A Pragmatist and Pluralist Inquiry in Global Ethics.* Oxford: Oxford University Press.

Hopgood, Stephen (2013) *The Endtimes of Human Rights.* Ithaca, NY: Cornell University Press.

Hopgood, Stephen, Jack L. Snyder, and Leslie Vinjamuri (2017) *Human Rights Futures.* Cambridge: Cambridge University Press.

Howard-Hassmann, Rhoda E. (2010) *Can Globalization Promote Human Rights?* University Park: Pennsylvania State University Press.

Hudson, Valerie M., et al. (2011) *Womanstats Project*, www.womanstats.org/.

Human Rights Council (2017) *Report of the Special Rapporteur on the Issue of Human Rights Obligations Relating to the Enjoyment of a Safe, Clean, Healthy, and Sustainable Environment*, www.refworld.org/docid/58ad9dd44.html.

Human Rights Watch (2016) *Closed Doors: Mexico's Failure to Protect Central American Refugee and Migrant Children*, www.hrw.org/report/2016/03/31/closed-doors/mexicos-failure-protect-central-american-refugee-and-migrant-children.

——— (2017) Russia: Events of 2016, www.hrw.org/world-report/2017/country-chapters/russia.

——— (n.d.) Business, www.hrw.org/topic/business.

Ignatieff, Michael (2011) *Human Rights as Politics and Idolatry.* Princeton, NJ: Princeton University Press.

Inguanzo, Isabel, and Claire Wright (2016) Indigenous Movements in Southeast Asia: An Analysis Based on the Concept of "Resonance," *Asia-Pacific Social Science Review* 16(1): 1–17.

Iriye, Akira, Petra Goedde, and William I. Hitchcock (2012) *The Human Rights Revolution: An International History.* Oxford: Oxford University Press.

Jastram, Kate, and Marilyn Achiron (2001) *Refugee Protection: A Guide to International Refugee Law*, www.unhcr.org/

uk/publications/legal/3d4aba564/refugee-protection-guide-international-refugee-law-handbook-parliamentarians.html.

Jensen, Nathan M. (2003) Democratic Governance and Multinational Corporations: Political Regimes and Inflows of Foreign Direct Investment, *International Organization* 57(3): 587–616.

Keck, Margaret E., and Kathryn Sikkink (1998) *Activists Beyond Borders: Advocacy Networks in International Politics*. Ithaca, NY: Cornell University Press.

Kindornay, Shannon, James Ron, and Charli Carpenter (2012) Rights-Based Approaches to Development: Implications for NGOs, *Human Rights Quarterly* 34(2): 472–506.

Kramer, Andrew E. (2017) "They Starve You. They Shock You": Inside the Anti-Gay Pogrom in Chechnya, *New York Times*, 21 April, www.nytimes.com/2017/04/21/world/europe/chechnya-russia-attacks-gays.html?mcubz=3.

Landman, Todd (2005) *Protecting Human Rights: A Comparative Study*. Washington, DC: Georgetown University Press.

Lauren, Paul Gordon (2013) *Evolution of International Human Rights: Visions Seen*. Philadelphia: University of Pennsylvania Press.

The Local (2017) Spain Welcomed More Refugees than Ever Before in 2016, *The Local*, 13 March, www.thelocal.es/20170313/spain-welcomed-more-refugees-than-ever-before-in-2016.

MAEC (Ministerio de Asuntos Exteriores y de Cooperación) (2016) *Candidate for the Human Rights Council: Spain 2018–2020*, www.exteriores.gob.es/Portal/es/SalaDePrensa/Multimedia/Publicaciones/Documents/FOLLETO%20CANDIDATURA%20DDHH%20ENG.PDF.

Marx, Karl (1852) *The Eighteenth Brumaire of Louis Bonaparte*, www.marxists.org/archive/marx/works/1852/18th-brumaire/ch01.htm.

Masters, Jonathan (2017) What Are Economic Sanctions?, *Council on Foreign Relations*, www.cfr.org/backgrounder/what-are-economic-sanctions.

Meijknecht, Anna (2001) *Towards International Personality: The Position of Minorities and Indigenous Peoples in International Law*. Oxford: Hart.

Meister, Robert (2012) *After Evil: A Politics of Human Rights*. New York: Columbia University Press.

Milner, Wesley T. (2002) Economic Globalization and Rights: An Empirical Analysis, in *Globalization and Human*

Rights, ed. Alison Brysk. Berkeley: University of California Press.

Montoya, Celeste (2013) *From Global to Grassroots: The European Union, Transnational Advocacy, and Combating Violence against Women.* Oxford: Oxford University Press.

Moyn, Samuel (2010) *The Last Utopia: Human Rights in History.* Cambridge, MA: Belknap Press.

Nelson, Paul J., and Ellen Dorsey (2008) *New Rights Advocacy: Changing Strategies of Development and Human Rights NGOs.* Washington, DC: Georgetown University Press.

Nickel, James W. (1993) The Human Right to a Safe Environment: Philosophical Perspective and its Scope and Justification, *Yale Journal of International Law* 18(1): 281–95.

North, Anna (2017) The Scope of Hate in 2017, *New York Times*, 1 June, www.nytimes.com/2017/06/01/opinion/hate-crime-lebron-james-college-park-murder.html?_r=2.

Nussbaum, Martha C. (1997) Capabilities and Human Rights, *Fordham Law Review* 66(2): 273–300.

———— (2000) *Women and Human Development: The Capabilities Approach.* New York: Cambridge University Press.

OAS (Organization of American States) and Council of Europe (2014) *Regional Tools to Fight Violence against Women: The Belém do Pará and Istanbul Conventions*, www.oas.org/en/mesecvi/docs/MESECVI-CoE-CSWPub-EN.pdf.

O'Brien, Cheryl (2013) Beyond the National: Transnational Influences on (Subnational) State Policy Responsiveness to an International Norm on Violence against Women. Dissertation, Purdue University, http://docs.lib.purdue.edu/dissertations/AAI3592829/.

Oomen, Barbara, Martha F. Davis, and Michele Grigolo (2016) *Global Urban Justice: The Rise of Human Rights Cities.* Cambridge: Cambridge University Press.

Park, Madison (2017) Police Shootings: Trials, Convictions Are Rare for Officers, *CNN*, 25 June, www.cnn.com/2017/05/18/us/police-involved-shooting-cases/index.html.

Pengelly, Martin (2017) Donald Trump Repeats Respect for "Killer" Putin in Fox Super Bowl Interview, *The Guardian*, 6 February, www.theguardian.com/us-news/2017/feb/05/donald-trump-repeats-his-respect-for-killer-vladimir-putin.

Posner, Eric A. (2014) *The Twilight of Human Rights Law.* Oxford: Oxford University Press.

Postero, Nancy Grey (2007) *Now We Are Citizens: Indigenous Politics in Postmulticultural Bolivia*. Stanford, CA: Stanford University Press.

ProPublica (2016) *Documenting Hate*, https://projects.propublica. org/graphics/hatecrimes.

Rabinovitch, Zara (2014) Pushing out the Boundaries of Humanitarian Screening with In-Country and Offshore Processing, *Migration Policy Institute*, www.migrationpolicy.org/article/ pushing-out-boundaries-humanitarian-screening-country-and-offshore-processing.

Rankin, Jennifer (2017) Russian "Gay Propaganda" Law Ruled Discriminatory by European Court, *The Guardian*, 20 June, www.theguardian.com/world/2017/jun/20/russian-gay-propaganda-law-discriminatory-echr-european-court-human-rights.

Reuters (2015) "War Zone" at the Border: Abuse of Migrants in Mexico Rises, *The Guardian*, 16 October, www.theguardian. com/world/2015/oct/16/abuse-central-american-migrants-mexico-border-rises.

Ribando Seelke, Clare, and Kristin Finklea (2017) *U.S.–Mexican Security Cooperation: The Mérida Initiative and Beyond*, Congressional Research Service, https://fas.org/sgp/crs/row/R41349. pdf.

Richards, David L., and Ronald D. Gelleny (2016) Economic Globalization and Human Rights, in *Human Rights: Politics and Practice*, ed. Michael E. Goodhart. Oxford: Oxford University Press, pp. 216–34.

Risse, Thomas, Stephen C. Ropp, and Kathryn Sikkink, eds (1999) *The Power of Human Rights: International Norms and Domestic Change*. Cambridge: Cambridge University Press.

―――― (2013) *The Persistent Power of Human Rights: From Commitment to Compliance*. Cambridge: Cambridge University Press.

Rodríguez-Garavito, César (2014) The Future of Human Rights: From Gatekeeping to Symbiosis, *SUR – International Journal on Human Rights* 11(20): 499–510.

―――― (2016) Trump's Victory Could Push the Human Rights Movement to Transform, *Open Democracy*, 10 December, www.opendemocracy.net/c-sar-rodr-guez-garavito/trump-s-victory-could-push-human-rights-movement-to-transform.

Rombouts, Sebastiaan Johannes (2014) *Having a Say: Indigenous Peoples, International Law and Free, Prior and Informed Consent.* Oisterwijk: Wolf.

Ron, James, Shannon Golden, David Crow, and Archana Pandya (2015) Data-Driven Optimism for Global Rights Activists, *Open Democracy*, 29 June, www.opendemocracy.net/openglobalrights/james-ron-shannon-golden-david-crow-archana-pandya/datadriven-optimism-for-global-r.

Rorty, Richard (1989) *Contingency, Irony, and Solidarity.* Cambridge: Cambridge University Press.

Rucker, Philip (2017) Trump Keeps Praising International Strongmen, Alarming Human Rights Advocates, *Washington Post*, 2 May, www.washingtonpost.com/politics/trump-keeps-praising-international-strongmen-alarming-human-rights-advocates/2017/05/01/6848d018-2e81-11e7-9dec-764dc781686f_story.html?utm_term=.d1ecdff332d1.

Ruggie, John Gerard (2007) Business and Human Rights: The Evolving International Agenda, *American Journal of International Law* 101(4): 819–40.

——— (2014) Global Governance and "New Governance Theory": Lessons from Business and Human Rights, *Global Governance: A Review of Multilateralism and International Organizations* 20(1): 5–17.

Sambo Dorough, Dalee (2009) The Significance of the Declaration on the Rights of Indigenous Peoples and its Future Implementation, in *Making the Declaration Work: The United Nations Declaration on the Rights of Indigenous Peoples*, ed. Claire Charters and Rodolfo Stavenhagen. Copenhagen: IWGIA, pp. 264–79.

Sandholtz, Wayne (2017) Expanding Rights: Norm Innovation in the European and Inter-American Courts of Human Rights, in *Expanding Human Rights: 21st Century Norms and Governance*, ed. Alison Brysk and Michael Stohl. Northampton, MA: Edward Elgar.

——— (2018) Backlash and International Human Rights, in *Contracting Human Rights: Crisis, Accountability, and Opportunity*, ed. Alison Brysk and Michael Stohl. Northampton, MA: Edward Elgar.

Schlosberg, David, and David Carruthers (2010) Indigenous Struggles, Environmental Justice, and Community Capabilities, *Global Environmental Politics* 10(4): 12–35.

Scotti, Ariel (2017) Two Billion People May Become Refugees from Climate Change by the End of the Century, *Daily News*, 27 June, www.nydailynews.com/news/world/billion-people-refugees-climate-change-article-1.3282594.

SEESAC (South Eastern and Eastern Europe Clearinghouse for the Control of Small Arms and Light Weapons) (2015) *Regional Conference on Effective Programming for Preventing and Combating Sexual and Gender-Based Violence, Belgrade, 27–8 October: Final Report*, www.seesac.org/f/docs/Gender-and-Security/Regional-Conference-on-Effective-Programming-for-Preventing-and-Comba.pdf.

Shafir, Gershon (2018) How Has the Occupation Occupied Israel?, in *Contracting Human Rights: Crisis, Accountability, and Opportunity*, ed. Alison Brysk and Michael Stohl. Northampton, MA: Edward Elgar.

Shaheen, Kareem, and Gözde Hatunoğlu (2017) "We've Lost Democracy": On the Road with Turkey's Justice Marchers, *The Guardian*, 30 June, www.theguardian.com/world/2017/jun/30/weve-lost-democracy-on-the-road-with-turkeys-justice-marchers.

Shapiro, David (2011) *Banking on Bondage: Private Prisons and Mass Incarceration*. New York: American Civil Liberties Union.

Sikkink, Kathryn (2011) *The Justice Cascade: How Human Rights Prosecutions Are Changing World Politics*. New York: W. W. Norton.

——— (2017) *Evidence for Hope: Making Human Rights Work in the 21st Century*. Princeton, NJ: Princeton University Press.

Simmons, Beth A. (2009) *Mobilizing for Human Rights: International Law in Domestic Politics*. Cambridge: Cambridge University Press.

Siskin, Alison, and Liana Sun Wyler (2013) *Trafficking in Persons: U.S. Policy and Issues for Congress*, Congressional Research Service, https://fas.org/sgp/crs/row/RL34317.pdf.

Smith-Spark, Laura (2014) Report: 40,000 Migrant Deaths Worldwide since 2000, *CNN*, 30 September, www.cnn.com/2014/09/30/world/migrant-deaths/.

Stern, Steve J., and Scott Straus, eds (2014) *The Human Rights Paradox: Universality and its Discontents*. Madison: University of Wisconsin Press.

Stobb, Maureen T. (2015) *From Rhetoric to Reality: The Role of Domestic Actors in Diffusing International Human Rights Norms*. Dallas: University of Texas Press.

Suárez, Ximena, José Knippen, and Maureen Meyer (2016) *A Trail of Impunity: Thousands of Migrants in Transit Face Abuses amid Mexico's Crackdown*, Washington Office on Latin America, www.wola.org/wp-content/uploads/2016/09/A-Trail-of-Impunity-2016.pdf.

Taimienova, Layla (2017) Kadyrov's Campaign of Anti-Gay Violence, *Foreign Affairs*, 10 May, www.foreignaffairs.com/articles/chechnya/2017-05-10/kadyrovs-campaign-anti-gay-violence.

Tate, Winifred (2007) *Counting the Dead: The Culture and Politics of Human Rights Activism in Colombia*. Berkeley: University of California Press.

Tharoor, Ishaan (2016) Trump's Victory Places U.S. at the Front of a Global Right-Wing Surge, *Washington Post*, 9 November, www.washingtonpost.com/news/worldviews/wp/2016/11/09/trumps-victory-places-u-s-at-the-front-of-a-global-right-wing-surge/?utm_term=.3f950ddb84cd.

Townsend, Mark, and Tracy McVeigh (2016) Migrant Death Toll Expected to Exceed 10,000 in 2016, *The Guardian*, 17 September, www.theguardian.com/world/2016/sep/17/migrant-death-toll-2016-syria-united-nations.

Tufekci, Zeynep (2017) *Twitter and Tear Gas: The Power and Fragility of Networked Protest*. New Haven, CT: Yale University Press.

UN News Centre (2016) "Unprecedented" 65 Million People Displaced by War and Persecution in 2015, 20 June, www.un.org/apps/news/story.asp?NewsID=54269#.WKTzqxIrJE4.

UNHCR (1999) Declaration on Human Rights Defenders, www.ohchr.org/EN/Issues/SRHRDefenders/Pages/Declaration.aspx.

———— (2011) *Guiding Principles on Business and Human Rights: Implementing the United Nations "Protect, Respect and Remedy" Framework*, www.ohchr.org/Documents/Publications/GuidingPrinciplesBusinessHR_EN.pdf.

———— (2014) Special Rapporteur on the Situation of Human Rights Defenders, www.ohchr.org/EN/Issues/SRHRDefenders/Pages/SRHRDefendersIndex.aspx.

———— (2016) Figures at a Glance, www.unhcr.org/en-us/figures-at-a-glance.html.

———— (2017) Refugees/Migrants Emergency Response – Mediterranean, http://rusconi.com/assets/Refugees_Migrants_response_Mediterranean.pdf.

———— (n.d.) Local Integration, www.unhcr.org/en-us/local-integration-49c3646c101.html.

UNHCR and Global Protection Cluster Working Group (2010) *Handbook for the Protection of Internally Displaced Persons*, www.unhcr.org/4c2355229.pdf.

UNHCR, UN Population Fund, and Women's Refugee Commission (2016) *Initial Assessment Report: Protection Risks for Women and Girls in the European Refugee and Migrant Crisis*, www.unhcr.org/uk/protection/operations/569f8f419/initial-assessment-report-protection-risks-women-girls-european-refugee.html.

UN Human Settlements Programme (2013) *The State of Women in Cities 2012–2013: Gender and the Prosperity of Cities*. Nairobi: UN-Habitat.

United Nations (2008) Unite to End Violence against Women: Fact Sheet, http://www.un.org/en/women/endviolence/pdf/VAW.pdf.

———— (n.d.) *The Human Right to Water and Sanitation: Milestones*, www.un.org/waterforlifedecade/pdf/human_right_to_water_and_sanitation_milestones.pdf.

US Department of State (2015) *Trafficking in Persons Report 2015*, www.state.gov/documents/organization/245365.pdf.

Wagner, Peter, and Bernadette Rabuy (2017) Mass Incarceration: The Whole Pie 2017, *Prison Policy Initiative*, 14 March, www.prisonpolicy.org/reports/pie2017.html.

Washington Post (2017) *Fatal Force*, www.washingtonpost.com/graphics/national/police-shootings-2017/.

Wire Staff (2017) Thousands Rally across India to #Notinmyname Protests against Lynchings of Muslims, Dalits, *The Wire*, 29 June, https://thewire.in/152470/protests-lynching-notinmyname/.

World Bank (2010) *Gender in Water and Sanitation*. Nairobi: World Bank.

———— (2012) *World Development Report 2012: Gender Equality and Development*, https://siteresources.worldbank.org/INTWDR2012/Resources/7778105-1299699968583/7786210-1315936222006/Complete-Report.pdf.

Yardley, Jim (2016) One Man in Italy Begs for Asylum, and Another Decides His Fate, *New York Times*, 10 December, www.nytimes.com/2016/12/10/world/europe/italy-asylum-refugees.html?mcubz=3.

Zivi, Karen (2011) *Making Rights Claims: A Practice of Democratic Citizenship.* Oxford: Oxford University Press.

Zonszein, Mairav (2015) Israel to Deport Eritrean and Sudanese Asylum Seekers to Third Countries, *The Guardian*, 31 March, www.theguardian.com/world/2015/mar/31/israel-to-deport-eritrean-and-sudanese-asylum-seekers-to-third-countries.

Index